HE WHO
LETS US BE

A Theology of Love

Books by Geddes MacGregor

He Who Lets Us Be
The Rhythm of God
Philosophical Issues in Religious Thought
So Help Me God
A Literary History of the Bible
The Sense of Absence
God Beyond Doubt
The Hemlock and the Cross
The Coming Reformation
Introduction to Religious Philosophy
The Bible in the Making
Corpus Christi
The Thundering Scot
The Vatican Revolution
The Tichborne Impostor
From a Christian Ghetto
Les Frontières de la morale et de la religion
Christian Doubt
Aesthetic Experience in Religion

HE WHO
LETS US BE
A Theology of Love

Geddes MacGregor

A Crossroad Book

THE SEABURY PRESS · NEW YORK

The Seabury Press
815 Second Avenue
New York, N.Y. 10017

Design by Nancy Dale Muldoon
Copyright © 1975 by The Seabury Press, Inc.
Printed in the U.S.A.

Library of Congress in Publication Data

MacGregor, Geddes.
    A theology of love.

    Includes index.
    1. God—Love.   2. Incarnation.   3. Theodicy.
I. Title.
BT140.M3   231'.6   75-15957
ISBN 0-8164-1202-2

*To those who are willing
to use their minds
as rigorously in their religion
as in their other concerns.*

Contents

Preface

THE topic considered in this book is certainly conformable
to fashion. That need not commend it. It happens also,
however, to be crucial for all who are interested in God. If
Francis Bacon was right in saying "atheism is rather in the
lip than in the heart," that includes everybody.

The problems the topic raises have been examined by
others. I claim only to examine them in an original way.
Whitehead treated them in his own fashion. Nostrums have
been proposed by eminent contemporary American thinkers
such as Charles Hartshorne and Paul Weiss. More recently
and from a different stance Thomas Altizer has addressed
himself to some of them. Many have found refuge in the
idea of what Edgar Sheffield Brightman used to call a God
who faces conditions not of his own making. That solution,
despite the protestations of its advocates, is inescapably
dualistic and therefore unacceptable to many of us. Even in
more theologically conservative circles, however, an uneasiness about the whole area we are to inspect has been for
long prevalent on both sides of the Atlantic. Toward the end
of last century, under the influence of evolutionary thought,
many felt the need to enrich their religious heritage by
reconsidering the implicates of the old credal formulas.
Kenotic christology had already provided a way out for
some. That preoccupation emerged in Lutheran circles and
later fascinated Anglican thinkers for some time. It was an
attempt, laudable but in the long run not satisfactory, to
answer some of the questions that were troubling honest
and thoughtful minds. When the philosophical work of

Pierre Teilhard de Chardin was at last allowed to see the light of day (by-passing, by virtue of the long prohibition of its publication, the jeremiads of the whole existentialist movement, nihilistic and religious), the optimism of the thought of that great Jesuit scientist captivated many. In continuity with the tradition of the religious evolutionists of the pre-1914 era, it came as a welcome relief in an age of despair. I, too, have considered in my own way the problems the topic raises, for example in my recent *Philosophical Issues in Religious Thought*, the second part of which (pp. 311–462) I entitled, "God as Kenotic Being," and also in a little book published five years earlier, *The Sense of Absence*.

The present book is a development of that exploratory proposal. I am now making a fresh approach to the whole subject by focusing on what is surely the most breathtaking affirmation in scripture: "God is love." Either it is nonsense, to say nothing of maudlin humbug, or else it is by far the most exciting statement about God to be found in either the Bible or any other literature in the world. If it is this, why not cut our intellectual teeth on it? That is what I am inviting my readers to do.

In acknowledging the helpfulness of my colleague Dr. Kevin Robb, who suggested some of the texts in, and provided useful criticism of, Chapter II, I wish to take the opportunity of thanking him not only for that but for the provocative encounters I have for long enjoyed with his learned and lively mind. To one of my doctoral candidates, Madeline Hamblin, I am indebted for calling to my attention some of the illustrative passages I have cited from Simone Weil. I wish also to thank Dr. Arthur Marder, Professor of History, University of California at Irvine, for unexpectedly coming to my aid while I was reading the proofs aboard ship between New York and Casablanca.

Geddes MacGregor

HE WHO
LETS US BE

A Theology of Love

CHAPTER I

Implicates of "God Is Love"

Love is God's essence; power but his attribute.

—Richard Garnett, *De flagello myrteo*

GOD is love: that is what the writer of one of the New Testament letters categorically states.[1] The astonishing utterance has captured the hearts of devout men and women everywhere and has even occasionally tempered the opposition of some skeptics.

It is nevertheless, for reasons that we shall consider later, philosophically puzzling.

So much has it puzzled the learned in the Church that they have generally declined to take it seriously as a theological proposal, preferring to applaud it as the passionate outburst of a pious disciple writing in the first century of the Christian era. They have treated it as we should all treat alleluias and other shouts of praise that are conspicuous for their exuberance rather than for their logical explorability.

The instinct of the learned has been right. They have been concerned to preserve the notion of the sovereignty of God that is an inalienable part of our heritage, Jewish and

[1] 1 John 4:8.

Christian, and they have feared that too close a look at an utterance so fraught with emotional appeal might mislead the intellectually unwary into a radically false understanding of the way in which we stand to our Creator. Yet, as I hope to show, the utterance must be taken seriously if we are not to put into jeopardy our understanding of the nature of Christian faith. Moreover, now is the time to take it up with the seriousness that the great theologians have always reserved for the central elements in the teaching of the Church.

What I am to propose flies in the face of a traditionally accepted, conventional formulation of Christian orthodoxy. By patristic, medieval, and Reformation standards I am technically a heretic. I suppose that had I lived in less gentle days I might have been eligible for the stake under the charge of a heresy bearing the fearsome name of Patripassianism. For as the French say, *aimer est souffrir*, to love is to suffer, and therefore, to say that love is essential to the Being of God is to say that in one way or another suffering is essential to his nature. That is to say something our forefathers would have declined to accept. They would have retorted that God, as Father, must be above or beyond suffering. If, however, we take seriously the declaration "God is love," how can we avoid the entailment that suffering is essential to the divine Being?

Since in all the great Church traditions, Eastern, Latin, Anglican, and Reformed, the basic norm of orthodoxy is the Bible, as it has come alive through the ages in the life of the Church, and since the Bible clearly says that God is love, I may contend, as indeed I wish to contend, that this affirmation may well be *for us today* a better expression of Christian orthodoxy than is the traditional formulation. As will become plain, my contention does not mean that God, in his love and suffering, is thwarted, or that he faces conditions not of his own making. Neither his love nor the suffering it entails can be subject to our limitations. Yet I would maintain that the One whom we call God must be *par excellence* dynamic, not impassible (as the classic theologians have held) but a God of anguish because a God of love. Indeed, his sovereignty lies in his possibility, that is, in the creative anguish of his love.

That my particular understanding of the nature of the problem is special and my treatment original (in however modest a degree) will be, I trust, self-evident. Nevertheless, as an old Hebrew proverb reminds us, there is no new thing under the sun.[2] The theme we are to consider, unfamiliar though it be to most people in our culture, is by no means entirely novel. About the time that William Temple's *Christus Veritas* appeared in 1924, there was a fairly considerable trend, not least in England, against the traditional notion of the impassibility of God and an interest in the possibility that, if there be a God at all, suffering must belong to his fundamental nature.

Temple and other theologians of the day were naturally cautious in suggesting this alternative. Such reticence was not less noticeable in the work of an influential Roman Catholic theologian of the period, Baron von Hügel. Though his status as a layman of distinguished ancestry helped him to express opinions that were discountenanced at Rome and therefore could not be uttered by priests or other official spokesmen of his Church (at any rate not within hierarchical earshot), he was certainly not one to be attracted to mere passing theological fads. Moreover, he was instinctively inclined to stress the notion of the sovereignty of God, an emphasis that was especially marked in his later years. Yet his essay "Suffering and God," published in 1926, the year after his death, shows how seriously he questioned the traditional notion of God's impassibility. At a more popular level, though with some very sound theological insights undergirding them, were the writings of a much beloved

2 Eccles. 1:9.

and certainly the best-known English padre of World War I, Geoffrey Studdert-Kennedy, whom the troops affectionately nicknamed "Woodbine Willie" from his practice of distributing cigarettes bearing that brand name. To a generation that had been through the agony of that most terrible of wars, "Woodbine Willie" preached that God is the greatest sufferer of all.

War was not, however, the only human experience that provided the impetus for that sort of questioning. The germ of it had been there since at least the time of Darwin and T. H. Huxley.[3] Many thoughtful Christians, while they repudiated naturalism such as Huxley's, saw in the biological discoveries of the nineteenth century the means to a fuller appreciation of the nature of divine creativity. The writings of Henry Drummond, Lyman Abbott and James McCosh exemplify the kind of outlook that emerged towards the end of the nineteenth century, notably in America.[4] Some of the most perceptive went much further, seeing, in one way or another, that such creativity would seem to entail a suffering on God's part that is plainly incompatible with the traditional understanding of the impassibility of God. The agonies of the Great War did much, however, to foster this *genre* of theological reflection at a time when, in some philosophical circles, what we now call "process philosophy" was being developed.

Both of these parallel movements, the theological questioning of the impassibility of God on the one hand, and, on the other, the philosophical quest for a metaphysic that would do justice to an evolutionary understanding of nature, might have gone on unimpeded; but attention was distracted from both by the rise of other movements. Among

[3] For a study of biological evolutionism *before* Darwin, see Glass, Temkin, and Straus (eds.), *The Forerunners of Darwin* (Baltimore: Johns Hopkins Press, 1959).

[4] For a description of the theological perplexities of the Darwinian revolution engendered in the late nineteenth century, see Basil Willey, *Nineteenth Century Studies* (London: Chatto and Windus, 1950), pp. 8–10.

these, three were destined to play an important role in twentieth-century intellectual life: existentialism in continental Europe, Marxism as it had been adopted by the Soviet party leaders, and not least, of course, the analytical preoccupations that were about to dominate professional philosophy throughout the English-speaking world. Much of the impact of the kind of thought that might have produced a climate favorable to serious engagement with the proposition "God is love" was lost. An anachronistic but provocative survival of the mood of the twenties is to be found in the work of the Jesuit Pierre Teilhard de Chardin (1881–1955) who, because he was prevented by loyalty to Rome from publishing during his lifetime, appears now as a voice from the past belatedly come to life and resounding in the ears of a generation accustomed to very different philosophical and theological noises.

We have not yet fully appreciated, much less have we adequately developed, the kind of thought that was adumbrated by such early twentieth-century prophets. We need especially, I believe, to re-think our whole understanding of the nature of the biblical God, the God who "was in Christ." Many twentieth-century writers have resisted all proposals that even suggest a possible threat to the doctrine of the sovereignty of God that is so striking in the Bible and in the thought of all biblically-directed theologians and scholars. Instinctively wise has been their caution. Not less needful for us today, however, is courage to question whether there may not be a better way than the traditional one of expressing the truth of that doctrine of the sovereignty of God in its full splendor. In taking seriously the affirmation "God is love," we are to be asking, in one way or another: in what does the sovereignty of God consist?

Love is a primary concept in the Bible. The Hebrew word *'āhab* and its cognates are used in a large spectrum of significations, as indeed the word "love" is used in English. It covers, as in English, not only a wide variety of natural human attachments ranging from the tenderly sensitive to the crudely erotic, but also the devotion of Yahweh to his people Israel, with all the care, compassion, and fidelity that are included in that devotion, and the corresponding response of the people to Yahweh their God.

The first biblical writer to give form to this theological notion of love is the prophet Hosea. He does so under the dramatic symbolism of a marriage between God and Israel in which God takes the initiative. God uses his love for Israel as the means of drawing forth the people's response.[5] Yet the analogy, striking though it be, is not quite adequate. While the love of a man for a woman and her response to it are rooted in a natural libidinal drive that is commonly expected to play a large part in fostering a happy marriage, God's love for Israel springs from no such drive or need but from his will, which is both sovereign and righteous. If the people are flagrantly unfaithful, God may choose to withdraw his love for them. In such a case, moreover, he would presumably choose to bestow his love elsewhere.

This last concept is peculiarly important, for in it is an implicit repudiation of the notion of capriciousness in God's love and the acknowledgement that, on the contrary, love pertains as much to the character of God as do the righteousness and the sovereignty that are inseparable from it.

Because, as we have already seen, "love" is an ambiguous term with a wide variety of meanings in Hebrew as in English, it is too vague to function usefully as a qualifier of "sovereignty" or "righteousness." These terms, however, might well function as qualifiers in an attempt to specify the character of the divine love. Yet by no means does Hosea explicitly say anything like that. His use of the analogy of love is poetic. He depicts God's love for Israel in very human terms. The righteousness of God, far from dimin-

[5] Hos. 11:4.

ishing or restraining the divine love in any way, intensifies it.
God's love is nothing if not generous and spontaneous,
unstintingly self-giving and warm.

The Book of Deuteronomy, by contrast, seems cautious
and restrained on the subject. In the Hebrew tradition it is
indeed the *locus classicus* for the notion of the supremacy of
love over law. Blessing seems to be understood as an
outpouring of God's love.[6] To love God and one's neighbor
is to keep the commandments of the law. It is in some sense
to share in the holiness of God. Because God has chosen the
people,[7] they are to love him "and keep his charge and his
statutes, and his judgments, and his commandments, always." [8] Yet in the Deuteronomic tradition God's love
seems quite measured. Not only is it coupled with the
notion of election; it is so closely allied to the concept of law
that the election suggests a moral preference. To love God is
an injunction to do one's duty. Love and the observance of
the law are so constantly conjoined that, in this literature,
one easily loses sight of the inherently generous and
self-sacrificial character of love.

Three Greek words are translatable in English as love: (1)
erōs, used, of course, for sexual passion, though also in the
general sense of what we might call libido; (2) *philia*,
signifying friendship; and (3) *agapē*, for which a special
meaning seems to be envisaged. Both *philia* and *agapē*
occur in the New Testament; but *agapē* is used for what has
come to be taken as a peculiarly Christian notion. In the
Pauline literature it comes to designate an *ambiance* created
by God in which Christ and his Church live together.[9] As it
nourishes the *koinōnia*, the fellowship of Christians, so also
it sustains the individual whose life is "hid with Christ." It

---

[6] Deut. 7:13.
[7] Deut. 10:15.
[8] Deut. 11:1.
[9] See, for example, Rom. 5:5; I Cor. 2:9; II Thess. 3:5; but cf. Chapter X.

makes possible a special kind of communication, a converse that transcends words. Lovers have never needed to be told that there is such a supra-verbal communication, and the Christian, "being rooted and grounded in love," is "able to comprehend with all the saints" and "to know the love of Christ, which passeth knowledge";[10] that is, it surpasses that kind of knowledge that is verbally communicable. No passage in the Bible speaks more convincingly for Christian faith than Paul's eloquent hymn to *agapē* beginning with the familiar words: "Though I speak with the tongues of men and of angels and have not love, I am become as sounding brass, or a tinkling cymbal." [11]

As we have seen, the writer of the first letter of John goes further. He states categorically: *ho theos agapē estin*, "God is love." [12] We might reasonably assume, of course, that that is what all the biblical writers are saying, each in his own way. Yet this writer, by putting it in propositional form, calls attention to the question, What are we to understand by the proposition "God is love," and what does it entail?

From the standpoint of much twentieth-century analytical philosophy the proposition "God is love" seems a paradigm of meaninglessness. Not only is there no ostensive referent for the subject, God; the predicate is so ambiguous as to make the proposition seem to say nothing about nothing. If one were to say "God is mind" or "God is the world," a contemporary philosopher hostile to the use of theological language might possibly concede, however reluctantly, that some sort of meaning might be attached to it; but of course a Christian would make the first of these two statements only with considerable reservation and he could not make the second at all. Christians, taught by their theologians, have traditionally made various affirmations

10 Eph. 3:17.
11 I Cor. 13:1.
12 I John 4:8.

about God such as that he is the Creator of everything other than himself, that he is sovereign over all his creation, that he is all-powerful, wholly just, and infinitely merciful. Skeptical as of course many might be about one or all of these affirmations, a philosopher prepared to be sympathetic might well treat them as presumptively capable of logical exploration. Yet even this sympathetic philosopher would feel obliged to treat the statement "God is love" as at best a joyful shout that might well be merely a devout person's way of saying "wow."

Long before modern analytical philosophy appeared on the intellectual scene, and indeed long before Hume or even Occam, Christian theologians seem to have been reluctant to take "God is love" seriously as a theological proposition. We have already noticed one reason for their reluctance. They may well have had other reasons, more similar to those that would prevail today. The claim that God is powerful or just or merciful must always have seemed more explorable, and therefore more useful in the construction of a theological system, than the proposition "God is love," which consequently has tended to be treated as an ecstatic, mystical utterance insusceptible to discursive treatment. That is not to say that Christians have neglected, much less that they have repudiated, the affirmation. It is, rather, that they have been inclined to set it above or beyond propositional discourse about their faith. The results of that attitude have been so consequential that I think we must inspect at least one of them before we go on.

Among those who espouse a biblical view of God, most will agree that the affirmation "God is love" lies at the heart of their belief. Yet that assertion is not only objectionable to contemporary positivistically-minded language analysts; it is also perplexing both to traditionalist theologians and to the devout. The latter have been taught for centuries how they are to conceptualize God, usually in one of two ways. On the one hand, they may first learn that God is loving, in which case they have then to be told, if they do not at once perceive it, that a deity who is loving but has no power to implement his love is no deity at all. His love would be impotent. In the jargon of modern politicians he would lack "clout." So, they conclude, he must be omnipotent, able to do anything he pleases. On the other hand, they may first learn that God is all-powerful, in which case their teachers will go on at once to soften the impact of that assertion of the divine omnipotence by imparting the news that he is nevertheless also loving. That news may well be deemed astonishing, since there is no reason why a being who is able to do anything he pleases should also be a loving being. Indeed, it seems *prima facie* unlikely.

Whichever alternative is adopted, a paradox emerges. If the hearers are prepared to follow the labyrinth of trini-tarian dogma, they may possibly find their perplexities partly assuaged; but they are more likely to find that such ancient solutions, however ingenious, aggravate rather than mitigate their puzzlement. The paradox will remain unre-solved, and the most obvious and notorious result of the failure to resolve it will lie in the challenge presented in what is traditionally called the problem of evil.

The paradox will emerge because, no matter how the teachers have tried to interpret the word *omnipotens* by referring to its Greek and Hebrew ancestors, the divine power will be accounted something that God exerts and is always exerting. I have some very limited power, and I use it, for if I did not I should lose it, as a wrestler would lose the strength of his limbs through neglect in practicing his art. Were I a despotic monarch or a world dictator I should have much more power than I now possess, and for the same reason as the wrestler I would take care to exercise it. The traditional model for conceptualizing God is that of a king. God, being sovereign, has what would nowadays be called executive power. Even if God be conceived as an artist working on a resistant if not recalcitrant stuff (as he does in Plato's *Timaeus*), the power he possesses and exercises is fundamentally of the same kind. At most we need only change the metaphor from king to captain. God, king or captain, has executive power. The uniqueness of that power consists in his never having to submit to anyone else's. As *actus purus* he is impassible Being. The paradox emerges when we set all these considerations against the affirmation that God is also loving. For though we may surmount the limitations of our notion of a love that entails need, we cannot overlook the apparent contradiction that God, who is *ex hypothesi* always exerting his infinite power over his creatures (that is, over all that is not-God), should also be loving his creatures.

Of course the notion that God Almighty loves his creatures, caring for sparrows and going forth to retrieve fallen sinners, deeply touches the human heart. It touches it so much that some may choose to overlook the logical puzzles attending it; others, intellectually more resolute, engage in the theological enterprise of trying to show that the paradox, though real, is logically explorable and that the doctrine of the Trinity, however outmoded the mould in which it was fashioned, succeeds in showing that the notion that ground and process are reconcilable in divine Being is not unintelligible. Not even the most ardent defender of Nicene orthodoxy could claim, however, that no problems remain. On the contrary, for all that Dante in the *Paradiso* and others have waxed poetic about the beauty of trinitarian dogma, and for all that a triune form fits a deepseated psychological preoccupation, there does seem to be something curiously cumbersome about the doctrine of the Trinity. For it requires believers who, like Anselm, seek to understand what they believe, to embark on a stupendously complicated intellectual adventure in order to make the combination of power and love that are attributed to God seem somewhat less unintelligible, provided that they are already sympathetically disposed to finding intelligibility.

The post-Nicene and post-Chalcedonian history of Christian thought and practice suggests, indeed, that the doctrine of the Trinity left a perplexing bequest to the Middle Ages. In the warfare against Islam it became the watchword of Christian orthodoxy. To this day in Greece and other Christian countries which, bordering on a Muslim world, are still fearful of Islam, the repetition of the trinitarian formula and the ostentatious use of the sign of the Cross are still standard means of displaying abhorrence of the Crescent. In the West we know well how both the Reformation and the Counter-Reformation fostered similarly chauvinistic battle cries. I hope I need not say I am far from denigrating the value of the trinitarian formula or proposing its abolition. It has played a vital part in exhibiting the peculiar nature of the Christian faith, not least against Arian and Socinian misconstructions. Nevertheless, as I hope to show, it may not say all that must be said today to express what it was designed to say.

The ordinary person, though he may be more able than the scholar to escape the theological and metaphysical conundrums the trinitarian formula presents, cannot escape the notorious puzzle: Why does God who is both so loving and so powerful tolerate the evil that afflicts his creation? *Unde malum?* Whence evil? That question has been posed in numerous ways. It was posed by Job centuries before Boethius raised it. In our own day it has been formulated once again in well-known papers by Professors Mackie and Flew.

The problem is easily stated: God does not choose, it seems, to intervene when his creatures suffer "natural evil," that is, the arbitrary effects of Nature. Big fish go on eating little fish; men and women are suddenly and indiscriminately crushed to death in an earthquake. The victim is just as likely to be a Schweitzer as a Hitler. More shocking still to ethical sensibilities is God's seeming toleration of the most flagrant injustice: the wicked prosper and the righteous suffer. Three solutions at once suggest themselves: (1) there is a defect in his love; (2) there is a defect in his power; (3) there is no God. The last naturally much commends itself to those who are already in any case psychologically disposed to be so persuaded.

I am going to propose a fourth possibility, namely that a profound misunderstanding of the nature of both the power and the love of God has radically distorted the traditional view of the situation. The power of God is not to be conceived as an infinite degree of power understood as the ability to do everything *(omnipotere)* or to control everything *(pantokratein)*. The unintelligibility of an infinity of such power has been more than once demonstrated by contemporary critics. The divine power should be conceived as, rather, the infinite power that springs from creative love. That is the power that is infinite, being infinitely creative and therefore infinitely sacrificial. The power that is at the heart of all things, transcending all, has been called by some agapistic. It is the power of sacrificial love. God does not control his creatures; he graciously lets them be. That need not mean he exercises no providential care over them. What it does mean is that the divine almightiness consists, not in God's possession of an unlimited ability to do what he pleases but of unlimited capacity for creative love, so that not only does he bring creatures into being to let them be; he creatively restores whatever seeks such restoration, so that the redeemed might indeed well be called a new creation, that is, a re-creation.

In the Synoptic Gospels Jesus never makes any explicit affirmation of the sort used by the writer of the first letter of John; he uses instead a poetic device for communicating the same disclosure about the character of God. His method, which we have already seen adumbrated in the prophet Hosea, is to present his hearers with traditional Hebrew symbols of God, Shepherd and Father, in such a way as to evoke gratitude and trust in God.

Gratitude for what? Piety might produce several plausible answers, among which a persuasive one for many would point to the assurance of salvation that brings the Christian his peculiar joy; but the answer to which I would especially call attention here is, I would contend, both radical and vital for an understanding of the implicates of the proposition "God is love." Even if God is as benevolent as Jesus depicts him under the symbols of Shepherd and Father, he could evoke in me gratitude for nothing more fundamental than what is commonly called "the bare fact of my existence." This reflection is of such crucial importance for my interpretation of the meaning of "God is love" that I must devote some attention to it before going on.

I wish to suggest that "bare" existence is the most priceless because it is the most basic of all possible gifts. There is nothing for which I could be more grateful, for every other possible object of my gratitude would depend absolutely upon it. I could not even be, as has been the claim of many saintly people, "snatched as a brand from the burning," unless I were first there to be snatched. What I do with the gift of existence, how much I make of it, is another question. Without the gift there is nothing to be made at all. Since this notion plays so vital a role in my own thinking, and is by no means generally accounted self-evident, I will allow myself a confessional aside that may help to clarify the nature of my intent.

I happen to be among those who have very clear recollections of early childhood. I can vividly recall, when I was less than five years of age, overhearing a conversation which, for all its casualness, confronted me with the then novel reflection that but for my parents I could not have come into being at all. I did not understand why, nor did I care; but a possibility that had not occurred to me before now troubled me. The conversation haunted me. I kept trying to envisage the alternative to my existence and to convince myself of its advantages. It would have enabled me to avoid the numerous irritations that plagued me. I noted that, for example, it would have precluded every possibility of my having a cold in the head, since one cannot have a cold in the head without a head, and one can have no head if one does not exist.

Being already so *intérieur* that I had to camouflage such tendencies (which some would have accounted morbidly introspective) under as heavy a smokescreen of bravado as I could then contrive, I tried to elicit the views of my elders by indulging myself in extravagant expressions of a distaste for existence. Even the most doting parents and relatives paid little attention in those days to infantile tantrums, so my precocious wiles were without directly profitable result. Then suddenly there broke in upon me a sense of the horror of the thought of my never having come into existence at all. Well do I remember that sense of horror, which was more like the anguish attending sudden religious conversion as conventionally reported than anything I have since experienced. It was like what the existentialists describe when they talk of *Angst*. It hit me hard: I suddenly saw "bare existence" as the *summum bonum*, the greatest possible good. In fact, however, the existence I so suddenly learned to prize was not really "bare"; it was already invested with a deeply religious quality.

Theological notions did not overtly intrude upon these soliloquies, for at that time mine were very primitive. Though my grandmother, an aged, vivacious, and very articulate Christian, had already given me extremely good theological instruction,[13] which I was later to appropriate, my theological opinions were still inchoate. I was forced, therefore, to obey unwittingly that injunction of Bonhoeffer that Maurice Maeterlinck had already anticipated in the

---

[13] I have recounted the nature of my first theological instruction in one of my earlier books, *Introduction to Religious Philosophy* (Boston: Houghton Mifflin Company, 1959), Epilogue.

preceding century, to live *etsi deus non daretur,* as if there were no God. What terrified me was that there might have been no me. I make no excuse for my narcissistic idolatry, though the magnanimous might permit me to plead my status as an only child.

I do not think I ever got over the existential anguish I felt in face of the awful thought that I might have been, so to speak, pre-annihilated. Flagrantly disregarding category confusions and ontological inconsistencies, I pictured myself in a dark anteroom to life, being refused the existence for which I begged. Even when I saw people blind or crippled I reflected that they might have been still worse off: they might not have been there. It never occurred to me to doubt, after my "conversion," that "being there" was the intrinsic good. That is one reason, by the way, why, in spite of the plausibility and even persuasiveness of some of the contemporary ethical arguments in favor of abortion in certain circumstances, I still find in myself a deep reluctance to diminish in any way my instinctive horror of anything that would terminate the life of a human being before we can even know what that human being would have become. According to Christian orthodoxy, one very likely candidate turned out to be the Incarnate Lord.

If we can grant that "bare" existence is good in itself, and then postulate the existence of a Being such as either the biblical God or the traditional God of theism, the notion that he simply confers that "bare" existence both on what I call "Nature" and whatever it is I call "me," and refuses to command or to control it in any way, becomes, I think, whether we accept it or not, at least intelligible. Nevertheless, as soon as we reflect on the notion of the biblical God, we must surely see that no existence that might issue from him could be "bare." It must be already invested with something of his own character. Whatever graciousness is needed to create as God creates must be reflected in the very nature of all the existents that are his creation. Even if we have the skepticism of a Voltaire about theodicies such as that of Leibniz, we shall feel no cause to reproach the author of our existence for not having provided it with all the ontological furniture we might have fancied. That would seem to me as churlish as my complaining that the free lodging I had received from a benefactor on a cold night was not appointed with an elegance commensurate with my delicate taste.

To say that the biblical God is love is to say that his creation is an act, not of self-expansion but of self-limitation. For the biblical God, being ontologically perfect himself as well as sovereign over and independent of his creatures, could have nowhere to go by way of expansion. He could have no ambitions to fulfill or goals to attain or projects to promote either for his aggrandisement or for his betterment. The only way he could go in his creative act would be a way of self-limitation, self-emptying, self-abnegation. That is what *agapē* would entail. Moreover, in conferring existence on his creatures, God must somehow endue that existence with some reflection of, or some potentiality for, his own self-limiting creativity, with all the anguish inherent in it. Neither things nor persons could be, in the well-known phrase of Jean-Paul Sartre, *jeté là comme ça;* they would have emerged already endued with those qualities that would make possible the capacity to develop the self-sacrificial power with which all existence, on this view, must be invested. Self-sacrificial love would then be an inalienable character of Being.

My contention, then, is that the traditional Christian model of the redemptive process is not only complicated by the peculiarities of Greek thought; it is vitiated by an inadequate grasp of the sacrificial nature of creation, which is intrinsically a self-humbling, self-restraining, self-limiting act. Even *my* creativity, such as it is, entails sacrifice and self-restraint. What then of the divine creativity that is the principle behind what the Christian Fathers called creation *ex nihilo?*

Traditional Christian teaching represents God the Creator as beyond both humility and pride. God then is portrayed as surprisingly exhibiting humility in the Person of Christ while remaining, as the ground of all Being, beyond such manifestations, which are seen as incompatible with his role as Father Almighty, Creator of heaven and earth. I would maintain that, on the contrary, both the divine almightiness and the divine creativity are implications of the omni-victorious love that *is* the character of God. That such a God exists is by no means self-evident; but at least the existence of such a God does not pose the insuperable difficulties attending the concept of God that has come to be traditionally offered in Jewish, Christian, and Muslim thought. At the same time it also does better justice, I think, to the biblical God to whom almightiness is traditionally attributed. Moreover, while it does not in the least diminish the wonder and joy of the Incarnation that Christians celebrate, it exhibits that central mystery of the Christian faith as the special manifestation for us of the characteristically creative self-humbling of God. We recognize as proverbial that even human love, if only it be deep enough, knows no barriers. That is the nature of the love that is to be predicated of God in an infinite degree.

In the next chapter we shall see why the need to provide for both *stasis* and *dynamis* in God was a problem for Hellenistic Christian thought. For us there need be no such problem: that unique *dynamis* of God that is the creative power in all its infinitely sacrificial self-humbling and self-renunciation provides all that was traditionally supposed to be provided by *stasis*. It also provides all the transcendence that the most anti-pantheistic of theologians could ask. God's infinite creativity, with the self-humbling that is its implicate, transcends all creaturely creativity, all creaturely self-humbling, all creaturely self-renunciation. Our human love would provide, indeed, an analogy, standing in relation to us as the divine love stands in relation to God; but God, omni-victorious in creative love, would in all respects transcend all his creatures, that is, all that is non-God. He would also be no less the ground of all Being than he is in traditional Christian thought, only the ground would be simply the divine love that Dante calls *l'amor che muove il sole e l'altre stelle.*

To that declaration of my general purpose I would add a note. In introducing my proposal of understanding God as the self-humbling power of creative love I intend to attack no traditional Catholic doctrine but only to show that the ancient formulations were necessarily limited by the structures of early Gentile Christian thought. I shall be saying things differently from the way in which the early Fathers would more readily have expressed them. Yet I am inclined to think that if they could be with us today they would no more object than would a Newton returning to hear of our contemporary understanding of space-time. To call space curved would have been wrong indeed for an eighteenth-century physicist, and it would still be wrong for anyone continuing to work within a Newtonian structure; but it would be commonplace for every contemporary schoolboy. In developing my theme I shall be doing anything other than renouncing traditional formulas. I intend, rather, to transfigure them. What I will say need call for no radical change in doctrine or liturgy. The Trinity would remain a traditional expression of what I take to be fundamental Christian doctrine. Collects would still conclude with the triune ascription, and the faithful would still make the sign of the Cross; but the meaning of such signs and utterances would have been transfigured. Indeed, I might even claim that what is most unusual about my proposal from a traditional Christian standpoint is that, in contrast to many proposals that are being made today in ecumenical Christian circles, only the formulation need be considered revolutionary.[14]

---

[14] Some may find such concerns unnecessary. Those who do not care about them may ignore my claim as irrelevant to their interests, while those who do care will be at worst untroubled by it and at best gratified.

CHAPTER II

The Ancient Greek
Tradition of
Immutability

It is not fitting for God to rush about.

—Xenophanes, *Fragment*

LONG before the great Greek thinkers were born, the
Greeks had already invested their gods with certain very
definite characteristics. Not only are they immortal, transcending the limitation of death that clouds all human
aspiration; their life is in every way radically superior to
ours. They are *rheia zōontes:* they live at ease. When they
choose to intervene in human affairs, everything they do is
done more easily than are human actions ever done. Homer
and Hesiod, when they allude to the way in which a god
does anything, characteristically acknowledge that, while
the action is not accomplished by a wholly effortless *fiat,* it
is performed *rhea,* with ease.[1] Perhaps, as Goethe suggested,
we humans like our gods the opposite of ourselves: the gods
we worship are our own souls turned inside out. It may be

---

[1] E.g., Hesiod says, in *Works and Days,* lines 5–7: "For easily *(rhea)* he makes
strong, and easily *(rhea)* he brings the strong man low; easily *(rheia)* he humbles
the proud and raises the obscure, and easily *(rheia)* straightens the crooked and
blasts the proud."

that the early Greeks, more than some of the rest of us, were oppressed by the cumbersomeness of human action. How long it takes us to get things done! With what difficulty we move from one place to another! How we are encumbered by our limitations and, above all, as modern existentialists have so clearly stressed in their own way, how we are mocked by death! The gods, by contrast, are immune from such limitations. That may be why they are so admirable. That may be why they evoke human awe.

Be that as it may, the notion is certainly developed and written deep into the whole pan-Hellenic world-view, through centuries of oral tradition, that the gods accomplish with ease whatever they do accomplish. Moreover, gods and goddesses, in contrast to men and women, are virtually unaffected by what goes on in the world. From the changes and chances that so much affect us they are immune. Of Zeus all this is pre-eminently true. In the first book of the *Iliad* we find that when he stands up none of the other gods dare remain seated. At the nod of his head that to which he nods is fixed for ever. At the nod of his head all Olympus trembles. His power is awesome: if he will, he can toss a god from heaven. What is most striking, in his dealings with gods and men, is the immensity and swiftness of his power. In respect of his own fundamental nature, what is most distinctive is his immunity from the effects of other powers. This distinguishes him even from other gods. While the goddess of love, for example, is very powerful indeed in her own domain, she is by no means immune from the power that other deities may exert upon her by the use of their own power-specialties. Zeus has to fight his way to establish his primacy. He has to deal with other outstanding gods, notably Poseidon, who controls the sea as Zeus controls the sky. He wins his supremacy not only by physical prowess but even more by shrewdness and cunning. His triumph is a triumph of *nous*.

All this is, of course, primitive and unreflective. There are obvious inconsistencies. If it takes Zeus some effort to wield his power, no matter how slight the effort may be, then something is hindering him. He is, after all, just a giant among pygmies: he does face other powers; yet such is the magnitude of his "clout" that only fools would dare pit their "clout" against it.

By the time we come to Xenophanes we detect an attempt to give a more coherent form to the traditional ideas. The power-worship remains unchallenged; but its underpinnings are buttressed by an attempt at a more critical understanding of the nature of deity. "Always he [*Theos*, God] remains in the same place, moving not at all, for it is not fitting *(epiprepei)* for him to rush about to different places at different times." [2] Then in what critical scholars take to be a continuation of that utterance, he goes on: "for utterly without effort he makes to tremble *(kradainei)* all things by the thought of his mind." [3] We can even see a change in Greek art. Before Xenophanes the gods rushed about leaping or, as in the case of Zeus, sending forth thunderbolts; after Xenophanes they tend more and more to be enthroned. The advance in the conceptualization is clear: no physical exertion is any longer needed, not even a nod. What the one supreme God [4] decrees in his mind is thereby accomplished, without as much as a wave of his sceptre or even a nod of his head. We should carefully notice, however, that Xenophanes, far from modifying the ancient epic tradition, is really reinforcing it. If he is critical, he is critical not of the notion of power in Zeus but of the inadequate way in which Homer and Hesiod have exhibited it. As a quantum physicist might say "the world I am showing you is not less but more wonderful than it has been portrayed by Newtonian physics," so Xenophanes, far from

[2] Xenophanes, *Fragment* 26.
[3] Xenophanes, *Fragment* 25.
[4] *Heis theos* . . . *megistos* ("one god . . . supreme").

undermining what the votaries of the old tradition of power-worship have always believed, is really strengthening and consolidating that belief.

Professor Eric Havelock, in describing how Xenophanes corrects Hesiod's account of the nature of Zeus, suggests that probably the main thrust of Xenophanes at this point is to assert that the power of Zeus, though not to be understood anthropomorphically, is unique.[5] Havelock, in recounting how, in Hesiod's *Theogony*, Zeus attains his pre-eminence in the pantheon by superior intelligence, points out that Zeus, after tremendous physical struggles and exhausting battle,

> in person moves from Olympus and hurls his bolts. The shock nearly convulses earth and firmament as the gods collide. Earthquake and windstorm accompany the discharge of Zeus' shafts. As the Titans are finally secured in Tartarus, the poet again reminds us that it is the counsels of Zeus which have achieved this. Zeus faces one last challenge, from Typhoeus, and again it is his intelligence that discerns the danger. After similar physical exertions, including a leap from Olympus, he vanquishes his last adversary. The labour of the gods, adds the poet, was now completed, and Zeus is "elected" or "nominated" king at last, a consummation once more achieved through the aid of intelligence.

When the surviving lines, admittedly few, in which Xenophanes records his "theology" are compared with this Hesiodic account, it is difficult to resist two conclusions. On the one hand, when the philosopher asserts the primacy of the intelligence of one god, as a factor central to the successful exercise of power, he is being guided by Hesiod's assertion of the vital importance of intelligence as a quality of Zeus' own nature and

---

[5] On the relation between poetry and philosophy in early Greek thought, see J. P. Hershbell, "The Idea of Strife in Early Greek Thought" in *The Personalist*, Vol. 55, No. 3 (1974), pp. 205–215. Professor Hershbell sees in the very term "Presocratics" what he calls "a kind of historical falsehood."

as an instrument of his success in three crucial contests. On the other hand, the philosopher, in denying that this exercise of power involves any labour or movement from place to place, is explicitly correcting Hesiod's narrative, and demanding that so far at least as Zeus is concerned, he cease to be a physical agent achieving his will through physical acts. Xenophanes is as anxious as Hesiod to assert the supremacy of this god. But he probably intends also to correct Hesiod by asserting that this god's power is unique and also not anthropomorphic. The role of other gods and allies in the struggle therefore disappears. In fact, comparing another statement of the philosopher already noticed, we conclude that he intended to suggest that there never was a struggle. The epic story disappears, to be replaced by a statement of cosmic control exercised somehow outside events, through sheer thought.[6]

The account of Zeus' methods has changed. The worship of his power is not only undiminished; it is reinforced.

Behind the whole Homeric pantheon lay an even more blatant and fundamental power-worship. For there is an older way of acknowledging and worshipping power: the *daimon*, which is a neutral animistic force. Mother Nature is a paradigmatic example; but she is by no means alone. *Daimones* abound. Myth and cult testify that, for instance, the abominable Keres (winged beings that bring disease and plague, old age and death) not only are rooted in the very texture of the Hellenic outlook from the beginning but, with other *daimones*, resist and survive the appearance of Zeus and his Olympian cohorts. "The older *daimones*, even if vanquished," writes Professor William Chase Greene, "could well afford to bide their time; for in a later day, when the Greeks found their human gods all too human, and powerless to help them in time of trouble, it was the older *daimones* who became their deliverers in the religious

---

[6] Eric A. Havelock, "Pre-Literacy and the Pre-Socratics" in *Institute of Classical Studies (University of London) Bulletin* No. 13, 1966, pp. 53f.

revival of the mystery cults." [7] The mystical revival of the sixth century before Christ had its roots in that pre-Homeric worship of natural powers. That old religion, rooted in the immemorial past, was revived, of course, "under special forms that had entered Greece chiefly after the Homeric age: the cults of Eleusis, of Dionysus, and of the Orphic and Pythagorean sects." [8] The guise may change; the worship of power is perennial. So central is the notion of power that no matter how it be allied with pride or violence *(hybris)*, no matter how much evil comes in its train, it is still worshipped and seen above all in Zeus, supreme among the gods:

> Father Zeus, they say thou art above all in wisdom, whether men or gods, and all these things arise from thee. What strange favor this is that thou showest to insolent men, these Trojans, whose might is ever wanton . . . .[9]

Even when every moral instinct is offended in the conduct of the gods, and even when men feel they must reproach them, none can deny their power, especially that of Zeus, and *therefore* is he worshipped above all other gods.

Even the gods are shocked at the apparent exaltation of brute force and undervaluation of justice, to say nothing of kindliness and compassion. At the outset of the fifth book of the *Odyssey*, Athene addresses Zeus the high-thundering One and the other deities assembled with him in council:

> Father Zeus, and you happy ever-living Gods: henceforth let no sceptred king study to be kindly or gentle, or to ensue justice and equity. It profits more to be harsh and unseemly in act. Divine Odysseus was a clement and fatherly king; but no one of

[7] W. C. Greene, *Moira* (New York: Harper Torchbooks, 1963), p. 11. The original edition was published by Harvard University Press, 1944.

[8] Ibid., p. 49.

[9] *Iliad* 13,631–634. Translation by A. H. Chase and W. G. Perry, Jr., *The Iliad of Homer* (New York; Bantam Books, 1972, p. 217.

the men, his subjects, remembers it of him for good: while fate
has abandoned him to languish sorely in Lady Calypso's island,
kept there by her high hand, a prisoner in her house. . . .[10]

Zeus is closely connected with Moira (Fate); but the
relation is imprecise. Sometimes Moira stands over against
him; sometimes he gives expression to Moira. In Homer
human destiny is sometimes spun by Moira, sometimes by
the gods. By the time of Hesiod, Moira has become a
plurality: the Moirai, the Fates, are depicted as super-
women who predestine human lives.[11] So, in Homer, "Zeus
weighs the fates, just as other objects are weighed: to
ascertain their weight. When the lot containing death sinks,
Zeus knows whose fate it is to die. This by no means implies
that he is subject to a power, but rather that there exists an
order to which he conforms. The weight of a commodity is
not determined by a power, but is conceived as a quality
inherent in the very structure of matter." [12] True, we must
be careful not to read into the ancient poets a logic or a
systematic coherence they could not be expected to
achieve; but the popular worship of power, to which they
give expression, is unambiguous.

The conjunction of power and impassibility (insuscepti-
bility to suffering) develops gradually. The religious ideas of
the poets are at first unsystematic, not to say inchoate; but
even before the philosophers intrude their critical dispar-
agement of the poetic inconsistencies, the poets themselves
do what they can to bring coherence to their picture. We
have already seen that Xenophanes does not think it is
fitting *(epiprepei)* for a god to rush about in the course of
implementing his will. Why? Human heroes are admired for

[10] From T. E. Lawrence's translation: T. E. Shaw, *The Odyssey of Homer*
(London: Oxford University Press, 1932), p. 69.

[11] Hesiod, *Theogony* 217ff.

[12] E. Ehnmark, *The Idea of God in Homer* (Uppsala, 1935), p. 78, as quoted in
W. C. Greene, *Moira*, p. 16.

the vigor of their action as they stride through their glorious page of history. Is not the conqueror all the more to be admired when he races his steed right into the enemy's line and swoops down upon his foe, slaying him with a splendid flourish of his sword? Would not he seem by comparison a feeble shadow of a man if, instead, he stayed home and, while calmly sipping his wine, cast a spell upon his adversary? Probably yes, till one reflects on what is implied in the kind of power that is worshipped. The god, in doing things easily *(rhea)*, exhibits the true nature of his power. He excels over mortals not merely in having a stronger arm but in having one that is so functionally superior in every way that it does, as we might say, "a better job," and so, like an experienced professional compared with a clumsy amateur, he expends far less energy. A cognate notion is found in Deutero-Isaiah, to whom modern biblical scholars attribute Isaiah 40–55, which they date about 550–540 B.C.:

> *those who hope in Yahweh renew their strength,*
> *they put out wings like eagles,*
> *They run and do not grow weary,*
> *walk and never tire.*[13]

The Hebrew prophet is telling his hearers that if they put their trust in Yahweh something of the effortlessness of Yahweh will be infused into them. They will have the wisdom of old heads and the vitality of young shoulders. The early Greek gods, though they do not grow feeble with age as do mortals, have the wisdom of old age conjoined with the vigor of youth; therefore (unlike youth, which wastes its strength) they are able to make the most economical use of their vigor.

From such considerations we have not a long way to go to

[13] Isa. 40:31 (JB).

reach the conclusion that Zeus, far from flashing a more splendid sword than anyone else, need not even flicker an eyelid. The bare thought in his mind is enough to establish his decree for ever. He need not move at all. Strictly, what is immutable should be impassible. That would seem to be already the logical consequence of power-worship according to the perennial Greek model; nevertheless, it takes a long time to work it out like that as Parmenides and certainly Plato eventually do. So in the poets the gods do suffer. Their suffering, however, is radically different from human suffering. Here we must bear in mind Homer's understanding of the nature of man. We mortals do not really *do* anything at all. As a contemporary scholar succinctly states the situation: in Homer "There are personal fates, but no personal achievements." [14] Far from my being, in W. E. Henley's well-known words "the master of my fate . . . the captain of my soul," I am but the channel through which divine forces flow. The divine machinery is at work in me. There is nothing I can do. [15]

By the time of Aeschylus (525–456 B.C.) the divine role is still by no means clear. Zeus is mentioned along with Might and Right: "May Might and Right, and sovereign Zeus, as third, be my helpers." [16] The immutability of Zeus, however, is becoming much more definite. He "hurls mortals in destruction from their high-towered expectations, but puts forth no force: everything of gods is without toil. Sitting, he nevertheless at once accomplishes his thought, somehow,

[14] Bruno Snell. *The Discovery of Mind*, trans. T. G. Rosenmeyer, (Cambridge, Mass.: Harvard University Press, 1953), p. 61.

[15] We may note in passing how far removed such a view is from the implicates of karmic doctrine in the religion of India and its Buddhist offshoots. For there, though the *samsāra* or chain of rebirth is under the karmic law, the individual can change his personal karma by his free choice. The individual is subject to karmic law; but he is anything other than at the mercy of fate.

[16] Aeschylus, *Choephoroe* 244: *Kratos te kai Dikē syn tō tritō pantōn megisto Zēni syggenoito soi.*

from his holy resting-place." [17] Aeschylus is apparently puzzled how all this works, for in the Greek text the enclitic adverb *pōs* ("somehow," "in some way or other") is used in respect to the doings of Zeus. How in his aloof immutability he accomplishes the exercise of his almightiness is a mystery; yet that seems how things must be. In any case, poets are not geared to the resolution of such problems. As we shall see, all comes together eventually in Plato, and then Aristotle formulates out of it a philosophical dogma which, more than a millennium later, served or disserved Christian theology.

Plato, however, is not the thinker to whom we must attribute the crystallization of the tradition. The proper recipient of our recognition is Parmenides. For Plato, rightly or wrongly, conceives his own task as an attempt to mitigate here, as elsewhere, what he takes to be the rigidity of the Parmenidean solution to the puzzles bequeathed by the poets. In the Way of Truth, Parmenides affirms his view that the One Being, reality itself, is not *ateleutēton*, incomplete. It has no lack of anything. For "it is not right for Being to be incomplete, for it is not in need; if it were it would need all." [18] That, according to Parmenides, entails its immutability. He thinks it obvious that a perfect being could have no reason to change or move about. Parmenides takes an already accepted theological tradition in popular Greek religion and carries it further; but, like Heidegger in our own time, he scrupulously avoids calling Being a god. He evidently wanted to avoid what we might call theological associations. Moreover, Being, as perfect, must be limited.

---

[17] Aeschylus, *The Suppliants* 96–103. Translation by G. S. Kirk in G. S. Kirk and J. E. Raven, *The Presocratic Philosophers* (New York: Cambridge University Press, 1957), p. 171: *iaptei d' elpidōn aph' hypsipyrgōn panōleis brotous, bian d' outin' exoplizei. pan aponon daimoniōn. hēmenos hon phronēma pōs autothen exepraxen empas hedranōn aph' hagnōn.*

[18] Parmenides, *Fragment* VIII, 32f. Translation by Leonardo Tarán, *Parmenides* (Princeton, N.J.: Princeton University Press, 1965), p. 86. The Greek reads: *houneken ouk ateleutēton to eon themis einai.*

Parmenides shared the typical Greek dislike of formlessness.[19] What is complete *(teleios)* cannot be endless. It must have *telos*. *Telos* is implied in *teleios*.

Parmenides says that Moira forces Being to be *akinēton;* therefore movement is merely the name of a fiction: it cannot designate any reality.[20] How precisely the first part of Parmenides' poem, the Way of Truth, is related to the second part, the Way of Seeming, is controversial. Tarán states the problem as follows: "According to the first [part of the poem], what exists can have no characteristic except just Being, the reason for this is that non-Being is inconceivable and a *tertium quid* between Being and non-Being impossible. . . . If this is the doctrine of Parmenides, why does the goddess continue her discourse describing and even apparently explaining what she had already declared to be non-existent?"[21]

There are certainly difficulties in the interpretation of Parmenides. Nevertheless, what is important for us is how he was understood by Plato and Aristotle. For Plato, in seeing Parmenides as a philosophical challenge that had to be met, brought into focus the whole Greek tradition about the immutability and impassibility of God and attacked it head on. Whether his interpretation of Parmenides was right or wrong does not affect our present inquiry. Parmenides certainly saw what the philosophical difficulties were. His precise conclusion is beside the point for us. He indubitably took the whole question very seriously as the major philosophical problem demanding a solution, and Plato inherited his concern. The basic presuppositions of the whole tradition, literary and philosophical, popular and learned, remained fundamentally unchanged. Moreover, Parmenides not only bequeathed a philosophical problem to

---

[19] But see Leo Sweeney, S.J., *Infinity in the Presocratics* (The Hague: Martinus Nijhoff, 1972).

[20] Parmenides, *Fragment* VIII, 37ff.

[21] Tarán, *Parmenides*, p. 202.

later thinkers; the ideas he was believed to promulgate passed into popular religion through the poets. So Euripides roundly asserts: "God, if truly God he be, needs nothing. These be the minstrels' sorry tales." [22]

Plato, in the third book of the Republic,[23] clearly rejects as fictions the poets' legends of the gods. In particular he makes Socrates repudiate the notion that God, "as many assert," is "the author of all things." He is not; only good things are to be attributed to God. Socrates also enjoins Adeimantus "not to listen to Homer or to any other poet who is guilty of the folly of saying that two casks 'Lie at the threshold of Zeus, full of lots, one of good, the other of evil lots.' " [24] All such dualistic solutions are to be rejected. The notion that God is the author of evil is "suicidal, ruinous, impious." [25] A little later he specifically asserts: "God . . . changes not." [26] So, though Homer is to be admired, "we do not admire the lying dream which Zeus sends to Agamemnon," [27] and so forth. "The lying poet has no place in our idea of God." [28]

Of course Plato wants to exonerate God from blame for evil and to insist that human beings have only themselves to blame. At one point in the *Euthyphro* Plato has Socrates defending the view that the gods do not make the right right by their loving it; they love the right because it is right.[29] Plato is trying to clear up ambiguities in popular and poetic conceits and he comes down on the side of the notion of a Being that is immutable and impassible. In the *Republic* his notion finds expression in the supreme Idea, the Idea of the

[22] Euripides, *Herakles.*
[23] *Republic* 379.
[24] *Iliad* 24, 527.
[25] *Republic* 380.
[26] *Republic* 382.
[27] *Republic* 383.
[28] *Republic* 382.
[29] *Euthyphro* 10.

Good which is the heart of reality. Yet Plato wishes not only to specify the heart of reality; he feels he must also give some account of how things come to be, that is, creation. When he does so, notably in the *Timaeus*, he seems to be trying to take seriously into his thought (contradistinguished from his use of myth) two different aspects of what we today would call God. When he turns to the creative aspect, however, he has to invent another concept, the *demiourgos*, to serve as a symbol for all the forces at work in the cosmos.[30]

He provides an account of how the divine artist, the demiurge, stands in relation to the cause that lies behind his creative work. The dynamic creator, in the long run, serves the static Being on whom even he depends. It is almost as though the dynamic were a translation of the static, a translation made necessary in order that the immutability and impassibility of the static be conserved intact, as we might make a xerox copy of a key document for working use in the office, so enabling us to keep the original safe in the deposit box at the bank. We cannot have the original kicking about: it might be lost or stolen or perhaps fraudulently altered. The xerox copy functions well in our various daily operations and transactions, and all the time there lies behind it the original on which it depends and without which it could not properly function at all. The demiurge, however, can no more be God than, in an economy that recognizes the gold standard, paper money can be the gold it is supposed to represent. For Plato has adopted into his thought and fully naturalized within it the whole ancient tradition of the immutability and impassibility of God. That is why, for him, the Idea of the Good might

---

[30] The *demiourgos* may be taken to be the mythical equivalent of *nous*, which is a more ultimate principle than the *psyche tou kosmou*, the world-soul. See R. Hackforth, "Plato's Theism" in R. E. Allen (ed.), *Studies in Plato's Metaphysics*, (New York: The Humanities Press, 1965), pp. 439–447. See also G. M. A. Grube, *Plato's Thought* (Boston: Beacon Press, 1958), pp. 162ff.

best symbolize God, whom James was to call "the Father of Lights, with whom is no variableness, neither shadow of turning." [31]

In the *Symposium* Socrates speaks repeatedly of the nature of human love. We have an overpowering instinct to propagate, because "the mortal nature *(hē thnētē physis)* ever seeks, as best it can, to be immortal *(athanatos)*." [32] Not only are our bodies constantly changing and becoming eventually old; even our souls are changing too, for we both learn and forget. Every mortal thing preserves a semblance of continuity by loss and replenishment. It does not keep itself the same for ever like the divine *(hōsper to theion)*.[33] Plato, when he wants to contrast the human and divine, makes use of the already built-in admiration for that which goes on and on like the river; but he calls attention to a finer point his readers might overlook: it is not the ongoingness of great rivers and old trees that constitutes immortality. Plato saw in his own way that the river is constantly in flux, as Heracleitus had long ago perceived. The old tree is only of greater longevity than we, so that we marvel that it has stood a thousand years while fifty generations of men have sat under it. No, the distinction between gods and men in popular religion is only one of degree. The *theoi* of popular religion are immensely stronger, cleverer, quicker and longer-lived; but that does not bring us face to face with the radical distinction that is to be made between mortality and immortality. The divine, if it is to be radically distinguished from the human (not just as a man twenty feet tall would be distinguished from the rest of us), must keep exactly the same for ever. It must *suffer no change.* That is what makes the divine qualitatively different from everything else. We may hear all this echoed in the familiar Christian hymn

[31] James 1:17.
[32] *Symposium* 207.
[33] *Symposium* 208: the divine is altered by nothing.

composed in 1820 by a young English clergyman who had been with an old man who, as he lay dying, had kept repeating "Abide with me":

Change and decay in all around I see;
O Thou, Who changest not, abide with me.

The contrast we are to see between the human and the divine is not that the divine lasts longer but that it never changes at all. Yet even in our mortal life something intrudes that in some way partakes of immortality: we yearn perforce for immortality no less than for the good, since love loves to possess the good for ever.[34]

By this time the Greek mind, encouraged by the poets, taught by the philosophers, and predisposed by its own nature, was thoroughly imbued with the notion that if there be a God at all he must be impassible and immutable. The next question was: if he is, how can he move anything? How can that which is impassible and immutable ever pour forth or send forth anything? How could it ever create anything or set anything in motion? Aristotle's celebrated answer was *kinei hōs erōmenon,* it moves by being loved.[35] This was an expression of his ingenious "magnet" theory. Plato's *erōs* has been raised to the status of a cosmic force. The whole of existence strives upwards, attracted by the divine, which remains unconcerned. Deity is totally immutable, radically impassible; but it draws everything to itself through the longing that everything has for God.

We might use, as a human analogy, the notion that a beautiful woman has no need to chase after her admirers, since they all desire her. Their *erōs* seeks her out. How, then, could God need to order things or administer the

[34] *Symposium* 207: *eiper tou agathon eautō einai aei erōs estin.*
[35] *Metaphysics* (Lambda) 1072b.

universe? By simply being God he draws all things to himself and holds everything together.[36] Such is the hunger of the universe for God that everything in it instinctively goes after God as surely as a pin goes toward a great magnet. Dante is likely to have had this Aristotelian model in mind when he concluded his *Commedia* with the line: *l'amor che muove il sole e l'altre stelle,* the love that moves the sun and all the stars. The love that moves them does so, not by driving them as a woman drives her spinning wheel or as a boy drives his top with a whip. The divine love is of such a nature that the heavenly bodies whirl round it as bees are drawn to honey. So God retains his self-sufficiency. What the Greeks had groped for from Homer to Plato now receives explicit metaphysical expression: God is to the universe as is a magnet to a box of nails.

Between Plato and Plotinus half a millennium elapses and the focus of interest moves from a demonstration of "what abstract thinking can do" to a deep religious concern. The Stoics exemplify this tendency: the ideal man is he who is serene in face of adversity and prosperity alike, the man who is independent of circumstance; for his resources are within him where resides a spark of the divine fire. Neoplatonism, as the school of Plotinus (c. A.D. 205–270) came to be called, was pre-eminently a religious philosophy. It was, indeed, a serious rival to Christianity and, but for the fact that it was too intellectual to be popular, it might well have displaced Christianity as the coming religion. Plotinus taught that humanity has a capacity for the eternal. The aim of religion is to enable the soul (which here on earth is a pilgrim, far from home) to be with its kin.[37] Our true end is a participation in the life of the immutable and eternal reality, that is, God. Our aim is to have a share in that

---

[36] *Politics* 1326a: *theias gar dē touto dynameōs ergon, hētis kai tode synexei to pan.*

[37] Plotinus, *Enneads* 1, 2, 4: *to agathon autēs to syneinai tō syggenei . . . synestai de' epistrapheisa.*

eternal reality.[38] The vision of God is the climax to an intellectual process: the ladder from the lower to the higher, the probe from the outer to the inner. That all this is a development of Platonism is easy to see. We cannot be too careful to note, however, what a special development it is. Christian and Jewish scholars alike were for long far too disposed to see Plato through Plotinian spectacles.

The influence of Neoplatonism on Christian thought is well known. In the West, Augustine, who had embraced it before his conversion, unwittingly carried a wide range of its presuppositions into his own interpretation of the Christian faith. He was also, of course, deeply influenced by the Bible as he knew it in the Old Latin versions (for he was without both Hebrew and Greek), and he had to modify his Plotinian thinking at many points. Nevertheless, in his conceptualization of deity he put immutability in the forefront as the way in which the Being of God is to be distinguished from man's. Of course he is not worshipping immutability in the ancient Greek fashion, as part of the panoply of power. We should not forget, however, that Neoplatonism had attracted him in the first place because its one changeless reality provided an escape from the seesaw of Manichean dualism.

We find Augustine, almost on the eve of this conversion, convinced that "that which suffers no change" is better than that which is changeable." His heart cries out against all mental images.[39] He beats them off; they pour in upon him relentlessly. He tries to conceive of God as a huge corporeal substance. Eventually entering, under God's guidance, into his inmost self, he discovers with his mind's eye, sitting, so to speak, on top of his mind, "the unchangeable light." [40]

---

[38] *Enneads* 3, 7, 7: *dei kai hēmin meteinai tou aiōnos.*

[39] *Confessions* 7, 1: *clamabat violenter cor meum adversus omnia phantasmata mea.*

[40] *Confessions* 7, 17: *intravi et vidi . . . supra mentem meam lucem incommutabilem.*

Through such introspection he "perceives" God intellectually *(intellectualis)* and, in accord with the characteristically Neoplatonic distrust of the senses, he is confident that
intellectual vision, unlike physical sight, is not subject to
error.[41]

We must bear in mind, when we try to understand
Augustine's intellectual mood and his eager acceptance of
the strong emphasis on the immutability and impassibility of
God that he found in Neoplatonism, that no one in his time
who was seeking a systematic answer to metaphysical
questions had much, if any, choice. Neoplatonism, as we
have already noted, was a rival to Christianity as a religion.
As a philosophical *system* it was unrivalled. There was
Stoicism and there were other philosophies; but they were
primarily ethical philosophies. Augustine was a man of great
metaphysical curiosity but no extraordinary metaphysical
originality. There were, in his world, no readily available
alternatives that might have stimulated *radical* criticism of
the fashionable Neoplatonism. When Augustine was ap-
plying himself to such questions, Plotinus had been dead for
little more than a century, and in those days that meant that
he could feel fairly near him in point of time. There was
really no one else in Augustine's world to argue effectively
and persuasively against the fundamental presuppositions of
such a school on a point such as the unchangeableness of
God, a point which, moreover, seemed to be upheld also in
scripture, though not argued there as Augustine liked to see
such matters argued. Plotinus had taught that God, if
nothing else had ever come into existence, would have been
unconcerned,[42] since he can have no need of any such other
existents. Augustine cannot agree that God is unconcerned.
He insists, rather, that God creates out of his goodness
(gratuita bonitas); but he accepts the notion that he has no

---

[41] *De Genesi ad litteram* 12, 14, 29.
[42] *Enneads* 5, 5, 12: *oud' an emelēsen autō mē genomenon.*

need to create at all. By this Augustine means, of course, that God is not driven by *erōs*, as are we, since there can be nothing outside of himself that could add anything to him or otherwise in any way alter, enhance, or satisfy him. Augustine sees that God must be free and that when, exercising his freedom, he creates beings other than himself, he communicates to them that same freedom to the extent to which finite beings are capable of it. God does indeed love his creatures; yet his love for them is fundamentally different from his creatures' love for him, and the difference consists essentially in that we need him while he does not need us, and were we to ask why, Augustine might well offer the reason provided by "philosophy": we suffer change; God is changeless.

Augustine himself recognized a philosophical difficulty in his own view. How can we who are in time and changeable be related to that which is eternal and unchangeable? God's perfection requires him to be completely changeless. It also requires him to be in a relationship of love with that which changes. Etienne Gilson, widely acclaimed the greatest twentieth-century interpreter of medieval thought, as he is certainly one of its doughtiest champions, sees the difficulty to be one so grave as to be insusceptible to any satisfactory philosophical solution, since the two modes of being are presented, in Augustine, as radically heterogeneous.[43]

Augustine, in his eagerness to exhibit pure, disinterested love as the essence of God's nature, while at the same time assuming the immutability and impassibility of God as the only "philosophical" view he knows that a reasonable person could accept, would be in intolerable difficulties but for one move: the Trinity provides a theological solution to

[43] E. Gilson, *The Christian Philosophy of Saint Augustine*, trans. L. E. M. Lynch (New York: Random House, 1960), pp. 189–196, especially p. 191. Gilson notes a Stoic solution involving an eternal cycle of aeons with rebirths and eternally recurrent new beginnings, which solution he rejects as introducing what he takes to be an even more fundamental difficulty.

the paradox that God is both immutable and impassible on the one hand and, on the other, pure love. Here, of course, he could feel on sure theological ground, since all Christian thought had been moving in that direction for a very long time and the Church had officially approved a trinitarian formulation. Through that formulation one could hope to see the nuptials of Athens and Jerusalem, the Word of God and the best contemporary philosophy. The doctrine of the Trinity was certainly a magnificent intellectual achievement in its day. We must now consider, in the next chapter, whether it is the best (or even a satisfactory) formulation in ours.

CHAPTER III

Is the Doctrine of the Trinity Otiose?

✦

When she felt the kill-weights crush
She told His name times-over three;
I suffer this *she said* for Thee.

. . . .

She caught the crying of those Three,
The Immortals of the eternal ring,
The Utterer, Utterèd, Uttering,
And witness in her place would she.

—Gerard Manley Hopkins,
Margaret Clitheroe

THE Trinity is never expressly mentioned in the Bible, except for a solitary passage[1] that every New Testament scholar knows to be a very late interpolated Latin gloss, forming no part of any early Greek text, or of the Old Latin in its early form, or indeed of the Vulgate issued by Jerome.

[Margaret Clitheroe, the subject of Hopkins's poem, was a butcher's wife in York who, in Elizabethan times, was put to death by having three hundredweights of stones pressed down on her.]

[1] 1 John 5:7–8.

That is by no means to say, however, that the doctrine has no *basis* in the New Testament writings. It was evolved in an attempt to try to make intelligible the affirmations of faith in these writings about God whom Jesus called Father, about God whom the Church proclaimed to have been in Christ, and about God whom Jesus had promised to send forth into the Church and whom the Church identified with him who had spoken by the prophets.

Grave as were the difficulties attending such New Testament pronouncements about God, they were aggravated by the way in which reflective people in the Mediterranean world tended to formulate questions about these difficulties. The doctrine of the Trinity was evolved very painfully and amid acrimonious controversy over a long period. Paul uses the phrases "in Christ" and "in the Spirit" indifferently.[2]

Early Christian thought often identified the pre-existent Christ with the Spirit of God,[3] so seeming to exclude the trinitarian concept. Tatian, Novatian, and others are ambiguous. As has long ago been pointed out, no early creed or hymn called the Holy Spirit God. Paradoxically, Tertullian seems to have adopted a trinitarian view only after having embraced the Montanist heresy, with its special emphasis on the Paraclete. On the other hand, Clement of Rome, in the first century, more than once used a trinitarian formula,[4] as did Ignatius of Antioch.[5]

Yet phrases associating the Spirit with the Father and the Son did not by any means necessarily amount to an acknowledgement of the doctrine of the Trinity as this was eventually formulated. The first official, conciliar statement of that doctrine as an expression of Christian faith may be

---

[2] E.g., Gal. 2:17; 1 Cor. 1:2,9; 6:11; Rom. 15:16; 2 Cor. 3:14.
[3] E.g., Second Clement, 9:5; Irenaeus, *Haer.*, 3,10,2.
[4] *Ad Corinth.*, 46,6; 58,2.
[5] *Ad Magn.*, 13.

said to have occurred when the Nicene Fathers declared that in the Godhead are to be worshipped Father, Son, and Spirit. The official formulation of the *theological* doctrine of the Trinity as three Persons in one Substance, three *hypostases* in one *ousia,* dates later still, from the Synod of Constantinople in A.D. 382. That synod went on to assert that all the *hypostases* are uncreated, being consubstantial and co-eternal, equal in majesty and perfection. Why three? One might argue that, for Christian faith, two would be enough, if indeed one would not do; on the other hand, one might also argue that if we are to have three there is no reason for stopping at that number and not going on to, say, seven.

In the labyrinthine history of the evolution of the doctrine one cannot easily escape the conclusion that, while it could claim to have some dogmatic undergirding in scripture, not only could scripture have been differently interpreted; there were indubitably also other reasons for fastening upon three as the formula. One need not exaggerate the influence, conscious or otherwise, of the triadic notion in other religions that have tended to conceptualize God tripersonally. That some such influences must have been available is beyond dispute. The Gnostic Trinity, which includes Wisdom (the feminine *Sophia*) with God and Christ, was known, of course, in one form or another; and age-old conceptions such as we find in the Tantric notion in which the masculine Shiva and the feminine Shakti proceed from Brahman, their divine and "neutral" ground, are likely also to have played some part. Concomitant with such universal psychological tendencies, however, must have been the pressures within the Christian Church, in the midst of the political and theological turmoil of the fourth century, to say something definite and metaphysically specific on the subject of the God-was-in-Christ theme. We should never forget either the reluctance of the early Christian Church to make such theological formulations or the enormous pressures, intellectual and political, requiring her to do so.

The doctrine of the Trinity, however it may have disappointed some, left most people convinced that it was roomy enough to accommodate their particular emphases without impoverishment. Theologically, Christians might have found much to be said for a Two-in-One God, and in the Alexandrian climate some might even perhaps have felt something might be said for a Sevenfold God; but in the complex circumstances that had arisen the trinitarian formula seemed to silence more questions than did any other formula that might have been a viable competitor. Above all, whatever its shortcomings, it was plainly inhospitable to Arianism, which seemed to many the gravest active danger to the apostolic faith.

The all-important affirmation for faith was that Christ is in no way subordinate to, but is fully God. Metaphysically, however, this affirmation was achieved by understanding God the Father as the Absolute, the final, transcendent ground, contradistinguished from God the Son in whom is God's relatedness to the world.

Only by a very artificial proceeding, a sort of intellectual *tour de passe-passe,* could that Greek metaphysic be squared with a scriptural understanding of the relation of God the Father to the world. For all the systematic splendor of the trinitarian structure and its uncompromising affirmation of the equality of the Son with the Father, there was in practice a damaging element. The ordinary, intelligent person, hearing that God the Father is the remote but necessary ground of all Being, while God the Son is the One who is accessible and susceptible to encounter, would hardly avoid the conclusion that the Son is, after all, somewhat less than the Father, though the denunciation of such subordinationism was, at least in part, what the trinitarian formula had been designed to accomplish.

Augustine, by way of surmounting this difficulty, propounds the view that the Father can appear, no less than can the Son. Citing the kenosis passage in Philippians,[6] he points out[7] that, according to scripture, there had been appearances *before* God had so "emptied himself, taking upon him the form of a servant." He mentions the case of Abraham, to whom, on the eve of the destruction of Sodom, God appeared in the form of three men. That it was God himself is clearly stated in scripture: "The Lord, when he had ceased communing with Abraham, went his way." [8] Augustine, paving the way for the curious combination of literalism and allegorizing that we find in the much later, Victorine school of medieval biblical exegesis, interprets the three men as the Holy and Undivided Trinity. He goes on to note the appearance of God to Lot in the form of angels, to Moses in the bush on Mount Sinai, and to the children of Israel in the pillar of cloud and fire.[9] He wisely concludes that speculation about whether such appearances were appearances of this or that *persona* of the Trinity is futile, since the Bible plainly intends us to understand that God the Father may appear as well as other *personae:* "By means of the creature made subject to him, not only the Son or the Holy Spirit, but also the Father, may have given intimations of himself . . ." [10]

Augustine's theological acumen is never more clearly shown than in his treatise on the Trinity, which might be more aptly called a treatise *De Trinitatis Unitate.* For while in accord with the intellectual fashion of the day he holds that the Father is to be distinguished from the Son as the cause of everything, and that through him the Son is eternally begotten, he also offers his celebrated theory that the metaphysical necessity for distinctions within the God-

---

[6] Phil. 2:7.
[7] *De Trinitate*, II, 11.
[8] Gen. 18:33.
[9] *De Trinitate*, II, 12–17.
[10] *De Trinitate*, II, 18.

head arises because God is love. Since God is by definition independent of his creatures, there must be something within the Godhead to make possible the expression of his love without having to provide creatures as its object, as though God could not be himself without his creatures, who would therefore come to be seen as needed for the divine well-being. Unfortunately for the later understanding of the trinitarian formula, these two quite separate understandings of its meaning and of its importance were kaleidoscoped. On the one hand we are asked to acclaim the Father as the Absolute, the ground of all Being, and the other *personae* as the Relatedness. On the other hand we are invited to see Father, Son, and Spirit as indistinguishably involved in the love that is the Godhead. The fusion of the two understandings is protected by the development of the doctrine of *processio* within and *missio* from the Trinity.

Procession is the emanating of one thing from another. The procession consists in action according to a principle. If the procession were to terminate outside the substance of the principle, it would be called transitive, and if it were to terminate in what belongs essentially to the same substance as the principle it would be called immanent. So we are to say that the Son proceeds from the Father by immanent procession; that is, the Father eternally begets the Son in such a way as to make possible the affirmation that the Father is the cause, the starting-point, or the origin of the Son. The Son is he who is begotten from all eternity and the Father is he who begets the Son from all eternity. To say that the procession could stop would be to say that God could cease to be, for that is what the cessation of the procession of the Trinity would mean.

So much for the interior life of the Trinity, the *vita Dei ad intra*. When we consider instead the mission of the Trinity we find a further elaboration in the classical doctrine as developed in the West: despite the maxim that the works of the Trinity *ad extra* are undivided,[11] we are told that the creation of life and grace in the soul is attributable to the Holy Spirit who is *sent (missus)* by the Father and the Son. This action is called the mission of the Holy Spirit. When the Holy Spirit comes into the soul, he comes as the envoy of the Son, who in turn is sent by the Father, who alone cannot be sent, since he does not proceed from any other *persona.*

Both the traditional notion of the procession and the traditional notion of the mission of the Trinity reflect the confusion of the two notions to which I have alluded: on the one hand the Absoluteness of the Father as *deus absconditus,* on the other the Relatedness of the other *personae* as *deus revelatus.* Nor are the difficulties confined to Latin theology; the Greeks, despite their abhorrence of the *filioque* clause, also account the Holy Spirit more especially the principle of human sanctification, being the persona through whom the Father and the Son act.

Since the notion of the Trinity was first developed in a Greek mould we naturally expect more illumination from the Greeks than from the Latin theologians. Our instinctive expectation is indeed right. In John Damascene, the early eighth-century writer whose trinitarian theology sums up the teaching of the Cappadocian Fathers, we find a new and singularly illuminating term: *perichōrēsis.* He uses this term to express the notion that the divine hypostases so perfectly condition and permeate one another that each one is invariably in the other two. This teaching is of immense importance for an understanding of trinitarian theology, because the Damascene, no less than his Latin predecessor Augustine, was peculiarly aware that a doctrine of the

---

[11] Augustine (*De Trinitate* I,4) says: *Sicut inseparabiles sunt, ita inseperabiliter operantur.* The Council of Florence in 1441 expressly stated: *Pater et Filius et Spiritus sanctus non tria principia creaturae, sed unum principium.* Cf. what some writers in the very different mystical tradition in the Church say of the union they claim with the Triune God.

Trinity could be satisfactory only to the extent that it exhibited the unity of God. The later Latin schoolmen rendered the Damascene's term *circuminsessio* (from the Latin verb *insideo*, "to be seated in," or "situated in," from *sedeo*, "to sit"), which waters down the perichoretic action to a mere cohabitation. The early seventeenth-century French Jesuit, Denis Pétau, perceptively protested against that mistranslation. *Circumincessio* (from the Latin *incedo*, "to move forward," "step along," especially with a majestic, measured pace) better renders the spirit of *perichōrēsis*. The objection that *circumincessio* implies movement and movement implies temporal action seems frivolous to me, since of course we are dealing in human symbols and human symbols inevitably have temporal connotation. We must ask, rather, what the perichoretic symbol is intended to symbolize, and that clearly is: the Godhead is not static but the dynamic act of divine love. The notion that this divine act cannot also be the ground of all Being springs from a presupposition not far removed from the simplistic and primitive one in which the ground of all Being is thought to consist of something like a saucer capacious enough to hold all non-God things.

If the force of the perichoretic doctrine is fully appreciated and its conclusions applied, how can we talk about the mission of the Trinity at all? The more closely we inspect individual cases, the less plausible the notion of mission becomes. When we hear of the divine *fiat* of creation, as in Genesis, we tend to think of the Father; if there is question of the actual carrying out of the *fiat*, we think of the Son, the creative *Logos;* and when we hear of the renewal of the earth we think of the Spirit of God, the Lord and Lifegiver: *Emittes Spiritum tuum et creabuntur, et renovabis faciem terrae.* If the perichoretic doctrine is taken seriously, as I strongly believe it should be, what can such distinctions mean? If the works of the Trinity *ad extra* are indivisible, what is predicated of one *persona*, one *hypostasis*, must surely be predicated of all.

Then why not say that the whole Trinity was incarnate, not just the Son? There is one fundamental objection: to say that would make the Father suffer, as did the Sabellians, who were deemed heretics and called Patripassians because their teaching implied the suffering of God the Father. Against these the view prevailed that the Son could be sent to be incarnate, but not the Father, because sending the Father would have been incompatible with his function as the Absolute, the ground of Being. The Father cannot be "sent." The more we probe the development of trinitarian doctrine the more we see that the cardinal difficulty, the one that reappears over and over again, has reference to the traditional notion that suffering is incompatible with the First Person of the Trinity, but not with the Second.

The notion that God the Father can suffer is incompatible with any Christian theology that is thoroughly entrenched in a metaphysical system developed in the Platonic tradition; but apart from one element in that tradition there would seem to be no particular objection to it. Those who look to the Bible as their warrant of orthodoxy will note that God is called Father not only because he is Creator but also because the characteristics of a good human father aptly symbolize him. Typical of the biblical view is the psalmist's assurance: "Like as a father pitieth his children, so the Lord pitieth them that fear him." [12] The biblical God is nothing if not full of pity. The obvious objection that such terms are anthropomorphic does not affect the argument. All such utterances are, of course, anthropomorphisms, whether they call God a strong rock or a pitiful father. The father-symbol as used in biblical literature seems to be logically incompatible with the metaphysical assertion that God the Father cannot suffer. Had the psalmist been able to entertain the

[12] Ps. 103:13.

view of God later held by those who in the third century of
the Christian era attacked the Sabellians, he might have
written, rather: "The Lord, strong and pitiless as a rock, is
the secure ground of all men, whether they fear him or not."
The psalmist was speaking, however, out of what he took to
be his experience of the divine pity. Presumably he saw in
his own way the love that Jesus characteristically predicated
of him whom he called "my Father." No doubt he saw, too,
that even if the love were no greater than human love, it
would entail the sacrificial anguish that Dante saw in all
genuine love, when he called it *terribile in aspetto*.

One might object that making predications of God in
terms of human qualities is to make predications of the way
he manifests himself to us, not as he is in himself. Some,
having in mind Calvin (or even Thomas as interpreted by
commentators such as Garrigou-Lagrange who underscores
Thomas's metaphysical agnosticism), might raise that philosophical objection. It has no *theological* force, however,
either for Thomists or Calvinists, for, as Calvin's twentieth-
century spiritual descendant, Karl Barth, recognized, the
force of such objections applies only to supposing that one
could get knowledge of God without revelation. For those
who believe the biblical revelation, the revealed God *(deus
revelatus)* is the hidden God *(deus absconditus)*.[13] If I
claimed to know nothing of God yet made affirmations
about how he appears to me, anything I said about God
would be merely a description of my own psyche. If we
claim to know anything of God, we are claiming to know
that the symbols under which we know him do point in
some way or other to his essential nature; they are not
merely descriptions of his manifestations. Thomas had
already seen this in his own thirteenth-century way. If,

---

[13] Karl Barth, *Kirchliche Dogmatik*, I/I, c.2, s.8. In English translation by G. T.
Thomson, *The Doctrine of the Word of God* (Edinburgh: T. & T. Clark, 1936),
p. 379.

under the influence of the Neoplatonic tradition, we were to talk of emanations of a God whose *ousia* (that is, his fundamental nature) were unknown to us, the question would still plague us: Why should an emanation of the unknown God be x rather than y? Nor does it make any sense to suggest that God, though he manifests himself biblically as a compassionate father, is metaphysically more like a rock. How could there be a compassionate manifestation of a rock?

These observations bring us near to what I take to be the central issue in the trinitarian concept of Christian orthodoxy. The model with which the enemies of Sabellius were working seems to be as follows: God is said to be both creatively loving and the ground of all Being; but to affirm both is a contradiction, an affront to logic. Must we then choose one predicate and renounce the other? Certainly not. Yet to call God both a rock and a loving father is like calling x both y and z where y is a solid slab of granite and z is a fleetfooted doe. Whatever x is, it cannot be both y and z. The answer upon which trinitarian thought insisted was in effect that God could not indeed be both a loving father and a rock, both the ground of all Being and the Incarnate Lord, both the First Cause and the Vivifier dwelling in and "breathing" into the Church, *if* the term "God" were to function logically as a simple term like "Julius Caesar" or "the Parthenon." What they proposed as the resolution of the paradox had been already suggested to them in some of the language of scripture: the term "God" does not function simply like that. God is *trias*. The term *trias* does not occur in reference to God, so far as we know, before it was used by Theophilus of Antioch about A.D. 180; but it provides a hint of what is needed for the logical resolution of a paradox. Then are there three Gods? No, that would be patently contrary to the whole biblical tradition. We say "Trinity" only to show that talk about God is not nonsense: the "Three-in-One-ness" of God, though a mystery, provides a sufficient answer to the obvious logical objection: we can now agree there is a paradox but assert that it is logically explorable. The various predicates of God we are making would be nonsensical if "God" functioned as simplistic people might suppose; but "God" does not so function. Such an answer could never have convinced anyone, of course, of the truth of the great affirmations of the Christian Church; but they could and did make these affirmations more intelligible.

No sooner, however, has all that been enunciated than another of the endless trinitarian conundrums raises its head. He who "sends" must be greater than he who is "sent"; so the Son, to say nothing of the Spirit, would seem to be subordinate to the Father. Augustine tries to overcome that conclusion,[14] which of course would have damaged the equality that trinitarian orthodoxy required. Yet if the Father is the Absolute Ground, the subordinationist heretics would seem to be justified.

Augustine, in his theory of the love within the Godhead, comes closer to what I think must be the way to handle a paradox such as that which the doctrine of the Trinity purports to resolve. Nevertheless, because of the metaphysical presuppositions underlying his fascinating theory, it fails, under scrutiny, to pass muster. That in order fittingly to express God's nature as love there must be more than One-ness in God sounds plausible. According to Augustine, the Father loves the Son as his "image" and the Son, in turn, loves the Father who eternally begets him. Thomas, indebted to both Aristotle and Augustine, says roundly that God loves himself.[15] That God should love himself is unobjectionable, for there is no difficulty in seeing that though self-love as we know it generally takes an evil form, it could take a good one,[16] and that in God its excellence

---

[14] *De Trinitate*, II, 5,9f.; IV, 20, 28.

[15] *Summa Theologiae*, I, 27,1.

[16] Cf. *Summa Theologiae*, I–II ae, 77,4 ad 1.

might well go undisputed. In the Augustinian trinitarian-love model, however, the Father loves the Son and the Son eternally returns the Father's love.

Why the eternal begetting and the eternal returning of love by the eternally begotten One? Were it not that there had to be an Absolute Ground, there would be no need for such a distinction. Father, Son, and Spirit would be identical and God truly that metaphysically simple Being that both Augustine[17] and Thomas[18] call him. Because the presuppositions of Augustine's thought force him to distinguish between Absolute Ground and whatever else can be predicated of God, he has to say, even when enjoining us to see the Unity in the Trinity, that the Father loves the Son as *other than* himself, and the Son so returns the love by which he is eternally begotten, so we are back to where we began: the Trinity is a way of trying to make intelligible the proposition "God is love" to those who have already a model of divinity that excludes the possibility of such a predication. Where the model makes that assertion obscurer rather than more intelligible, as is certainly the case for people today who habitually use forms of conceptualization alien to Augustine's, I think it may be properly judged otiose. That is not to say that trinitarian doctrine must be repudiated or even that it should be quietly abandoned. On the contrary, it cannot be so easily dealt with. It is inextricably woven into the history of Christian thought and has played an invaluable part in exhibiting the nature of the God whom Christians acclaim. There are many other reasons, moreover, why it should be retained in full splendor in the liturgy of the Church. There should also be made available, however, another theological idiom, another way of expressing what the doctrine of the Trinity was so laboriously designed to express. Christians might still sing

[17] *De Trinitate*, VI, 6.
[18] *Summa Theologiae*, I, 3, 7.

the *Gloria* at Mass with great gusto, as they sing songs about the Lord their Shepherd. They need not be inhibited in their devotion either because the imagery of the twenty-third psalm is quaintly outmoded for the millions in metropolitan areas who have never seen a shepherd and in some cases not even a sheep, or because the metaphysical underpinnings of the *Gloria in excelsis* no longer have the compelling force they had in the fourth century.

There are, however, two questions to which we should address ourselves: First, is there a way of expressing in an idiom more congenial to contemporary modes of thinking the notion of cosmic *agapē* that the trinitarian formula embodies? Second, while the doctrine that is embodied in the trinitarian formula is a classic expression of what may be taken as Christian orthodoxy *de deo,* can we say that such an understanding of God, when formulated in a contemporary idiom, is at least an intelligible and plausible notion to those who do not necessarily rely on the Bible as their sole or even their primary authority?

Simone Weil, that French genius whose thought is often very provocative in the study we have undertaken, has a proposal that suggests a novel way of presenting trinitarian truth about God in contemporary terms. As we shall see in some more detail later, she conceives of creation itself as an act of divine self-emptying, a self-withdrawal or self-diminution on God's part. "The Father is creation of being, the Son is renunciation of being; this double pulsation is one single act which is Love or Spirit. When humility gives us a part in it, the Trinity is in us. This exchange of love between the Father and the Son passes through creation. All we are asked to do is to consent to its passing through. We are nothing else but this consent." [19] She takes the Incarnation to be an image or symbol (*figure*) of the Creation. God, in

[19] Simone Weil, *First and Last Notebooks,* trans. R. Rees (London: Oxford University Press, 1970), p. 102.

giving us existence, "abdicates" and we can become in that respect like God by our self-emptying, our self-abnegation.[20] God does not exercise his "almightiness": if he did, neither we nor anything else would exist. God "chains himself down," to give us freedom, to let us be.[21] Only love can let another being be.

[20] Simone Weil, *La Connaissance surnaturelle* (Paris: Gallimard, 1950), p. 264: "L'Incarnation n'est qu'une figure de la Création. Dieu a abdiqué en nous donnant l'existence. Nous abdiquons et devenons ainsi semblables à Dieu la refusant."
[21] Simone Weil, *The Notebooks of Simone Weil*, 2 vols., trans. A. Wills (New York: G. P. Putnam's Sons, 1956), Vol. I, p. 191.

CHAPTER IV

Kenotic Theory and Its Historic Setting

Through the Uncreated,
Uncleft, Untrod,
Breathed for a moment
Sorrow of God.

—Amy K. Clarke,
"Vision of Him".

As has been argued, contemporary expression of the orthodox Christian doctrine of God may not be best served by the traditional trinitarian formulation. Before considering the development of kenotic theory, I wish to discuss some matters connected with trinitarian formulation, especially in regard to the formula provided by the Council of Chalcedon in the year 451. First of all, however, I shall say something about a radical divergence in the way in which the religions of the world have conceptualized deity.

Among those willing to entertain the notion that any concept of God is intelligible at all, there is a large spectrum of theological opinion on what such intelligibility makes available. Thoughtful men, whatever their religious tradition, recognize that no claim to knowledge of God can be wholly reducible to our human thought structures, even if it be reducible at all; nevertheless, they are compelled to express themselves through these thought structures, *faute de mieux*. Once we become attached, however, to a particular mode of conceptualizing deity, we are notoriously inclined to adhere to it with leech-like persistence, not to say obstinacy. For our present purpose we need not attempt any inventory of the possibilities. They are competently treated in well-known textbooks on the history of religions. I would merely draw attention here to two patently different ways of conceptualizing God.

According to one that has prevailed widely in the Orient and has exercised some influence in our own culture, deity is to be conceived as the essence or core of reality, the reality we are imperfectly grasping in everyday experience. That way of conceptualizing deity is intelligible only on the assumption that our apprehension of reality is customarily defective but may be improved through certain religious exercises, ritual acts, or mystical engagements. The difficulties such a stance must face in the light of modern scientific method may not be insurmountable; but they are very serious indeed. For instance, are those who take it able to say that modern sciences such as physics and biology lead us away from epistemological error and illusion and nearer to reality and may therefore be said to lead us nearer what theologians call "knowledge of God," or are they constrained to affirm that these sciences alienate us further than ever from reality, entrenching us deeper in illusion?

Be that as it may, the outlook has a respectable intellectual history. It is widely reflected in the Upanishads and is the subject of a very influential literature in the history of religions. It is characteristic of Vedanta. Both Hinayana and Mahayana forms of Buddhism have also inherited it, though not uncritically, and it has found in the Occident both learned interpreters and, not least in our own time, a considerable body of popular exponents. Its tendency is to identify God with the totality of Being and then to say that because our ordinary apprehension of Being is partial we get a distorted view of it. Instead of grasping Brahman (reality) we see only *maya*, a term used to express the illusory character of our apprehension. To this general metaphysical stance John Toland, a Roman Catholic Irishman who became a deist, gave one of his celebrated neologisms: he called it, in 1705, "pantheism," in sharp contrast to the deism of his own position. On modified forms of pantheism such as are to be found in Schelling, for instance, the German writer F. C. K. Krause, Toland's contemporary, bestowed the term *panentheismus* (English, "panentheism"). In modern dress, panentheism has found favor in some theological circles today, not least in Germany and in the United States, for example among followers of Paul Tillich and Charles Hartshorne.

Such tendencies reflect a religious insight and mood whose importance we should not denigrate. Plato, in his attempts to introduce abstract thought to a people still immersed in an oral tradition of poetry and myth, was not unaffected by the tendencies to which I refer, which had already found classic expression in the Indus Valley. In one form or another these tendencies were familiar to the Mediterranean world in the time of Jesus. In Jewish, Christian, and Islamic thought, however, pantheism has been very strongly resisted, not to say feared. These traditions, despite the great differences among them, share a common distrust of all such tendencies, affirming instead the view that God, as creator of all that is not-God, stands apart from his creation and, being absolutely sovereign over it, is completely independent of it. In these traditions, to seek God is not to attune oneself better, or to align oneself more adroitly, to that which is already confronting one in everyday experience. It is, rather, to enter into a different order or dimension of reality. In the language of Buber's disciples today, one does not experience such a God; one encounters him. He stands sharply against Nature, which is his own creation. Not all exponents of these traditions would be so uncompromising, of course; but this second view I have outlined is as typical of them as it is untypical of the upanishadic heritage. Orthodox Muslims vehemently uphold the position it represents. They account it not only consonant with but expressive of the very core of the biblical teaching from which Muhammad indubitably received much of his inspiration. It reveres and glorifies not only the absolute sovereignty of God but the omnipotence of his will. Everything is completely in his hands and totally at his disposal. If we were to say only one thing about God, it would be, on this view, that he transcends all things.

By the fourth century of our era, Christian thinkers, while clinging to that general tradition as represented in their Hebrew heritage, and renouncing its pantheistic alternative, had found, in the doctrine of the Trinity, a means of advancing beyond both. They did so by dealing with some of the special problems that were presented by the peculiarly Christian claim that God, the God of Abraham and of Isaac, had been "in Christ reconciling the world to himself." The claim seemed indecent. As a later generation might have said, it offended both faith and reason, both reason and common sense. Paul recognized it to be a stumbling block to the Jews, and to the Greeks mere foolishness. How could God, whom the Bible called Father and who in the intellectual climate of the day seemed fittingly identified with the unchangeable, immutable ground of all things (the "saucer-under-the-world") become anything other than himself? In mythopoeic language, how could he leave the Throne of Heaven unoccupied and go forth to pitch his tent among men, sojourning with them for a little while for the purpose of providing them with the conditions for redemption? It seemed as silly as asking that the grass on which the dew rests should become dew and then become once again grass. How could either grass or dew so behave, since dew cannot rest on nothing and it certainly cannot turn into that whose function is to hold and support it?

The doctrine of the Trinity answered such questions and others too in its own fashion. The very vigor of the controversies attending the doctrine in the fourth and fifth centuries are testimony to its relevance to the thought of the day. The doctrine answered questions well enough to have remained the official classical account of the nature of God as viewed by Christian orthodoxy. Yet there were many questions that it did not answer. Most notably it failed to answer those questions that contemporary philosophers of religion assemble under what is commonly called the problem of evil, perhaps the most intractable of all difficulties that theists face.

The uncompromising recognition by the Council of Chalcedon of both the divinity and the humanity of Christ and their unchangeable *(atreptos)* and inseparable *(achōristos)* existence provided the Christian Church with a means of limiting speculation. Christ was to be acclaimed both "true God" and "true man." So great, however, were the difficulties of Chalcedonian orthodoxy that not only some Churches, such as the Copts and the Ethiopians, have remained to this day formally monophysite, denying the duality of Christ's nature; even the Latin Church, though officially subscribing to Chalcedon, was never entirely happy, to say the least, with the Chalcedonian formula. This has been eloquently exhibited in our own time by Père Yves Congar, O.P., both in his *Vraie et fausse réforme dans l'Eglise* and to a more general audience in his *Christ, Our Lady and the Church*, where he has shown that the human nature of Christ was not taken as seriously as was the divine. Instead, a crypto-monophysitism permeated the whole temper of medieval Christian thought and devotion in such a way that the difficulties Chalcedon presented could be overlooked or indefinitely postponed.

By the time of the High Middle Ages, that crypto-monophysitism had so dehumanized Christ that he could no longer satisfactorily function as Mediator; hence the need

for a Mediatrix, whom medieval piety readily recognized in
Mary. I think it could be shown that devotion to Mary has
been almost commensurate with the prevalence of a
monophysite temper. We are left, however, with a question
of considerable importance for our theme: Why did monophysite tendencies so widely and independently prevail in
both East and West? Their prevalence is greater than is
commonly supposed. A judicious person standing outside
the controversy might well account even the use of the term
"monophysite" ("one-nature") tendentious, for it presupposes that if there is only one nature there is no need to
specify which of the two it is.

The Latin Church in the Middle Ages, for all the richness
of its theological and liturgical life, had a particular,
additional difficulty in dealing with Chalcedonian questions.
The Latins had never fully understood the subtleties of
Greek patristic thought. The more deeply they became
entrenched in the culture of a spiritualized *Romanitas*, the
further they removed themselves from the possibility of
understanding these Greek subtleties. As G. L. Prestige has
pointedly said of the triumph of Chalcedon, "the clumsy
Occident intervened as teacher in a matter which it had not
properly learned and did not readily understand." [1] The real
difficulty, then, was that while Chalcedon had very properly
set certain limits to Christian speculation about the divine
nature, the Latin world, characteristically literalistic, had
taken its pronouncements to be a final theological formulation. Latin medieval piety, often more sensitive than its
theological teachers, no doubt saw in its own way the
inadequacy of the traditional concept of God; but it lacked
the intellectual means of remedying it. Christ, whom the
iconography of the earlier Middle Ages had recognized as
the Good Shepherd, *bonus pastor*, had become, as Michel-
angelo was to depict him so splendidly, the eternal Judge.

[1] G. L. Prestige, *God in Patristic Thought* (London: S.P.C.K., 1925), p. 279.

Hence upon Mary was poured forth, with passionate affection, the adoring love that, according to the Calvinists of a later generation, they should have reserved for God.

Yet these same medieval people, the remoteness of their concept of God notwithstanding, somehow preserved what the sons and daughters of the Reformation, for all their heritage of Chalcedonian orthodoxy or perhaps because of it, were eventually to undermine: a sense of the ontological independence of the Creator, the One, the Being, who stands apart from the creation he sustains. The great theologians of the Middle Ages had indeed provided the medieval religious consciousness with a means of seeing in God the ground of all Being, the source of "all things visible and invisible"; but in the divine nature as medieval piety understood it there seemed no adequate answer to the great problems of human life. For the solution of these, ordinary men and women in the Middle Ages, including the rank and file of the clergy, had to fend for themselves. So with the quasi-official mode of conceptualizing God that the theologians provided came to be mixed a vast network of popular devotion that some comparative historians have found reminiscent of Indian *Bhakti*. The sixteenth-century Reformers, not least Calvin, were able, by invoking the authority of scripture above patristic writings and conciliar decisions, to uphold even more self-consciously the sovereignty of God; yet in modern "Protestantism," even in the most active and dedicated circles, there is notoriously a strong tendency to accept the humanity of Christ and shelve the notion of his divinity. To say the least, if medieval piety was crypto-monophysite, the heirs of the Reformation have no less often fostered a crypto-Arian piety that is even more alien from classical Reformation theology than were the more extravagant late medieval devotional practices alien from the teachings of Saint Thomas. In both cases the root of the *malaise* has lain in the perplexity, no doubt often unconscious, about the Chalcedonian formula that had been designed to put a brake on theological speculation whose profitlessness Nicene orthodoxy had already assured.

The christological difficulties experienced by the patristic and medieval writers had been already present, however, from the earliest times. Professor John Knox sees them as having existed in the thought of the Christian Church even before the New Testament documents had assumed their final form.[2] He thinks, indeed, that there was a primitive kenoticist as well as a primitive adoptionist christology and he sees docetism as an extreme development (eventually rejected, of course, as unacceptable to the Church) of early belief in a pre-existence christology. The adoptionist and kenoticist views would have begun as "relatively simple pictures": according to the first, "a man is exalted to be Lord and Christ," and according to the second, "a divine being empties himself of his divine nature and status and becomes a man. So simple is each story that it can be thought of as coming suddenly and full-blown into existence. The moment those who remembered Jesus recognized him as their risen Lord, the first story had taken its essential shape; and the moment he was pictured as having been pre-existent in heaven, the second story was fully in being." [3] Within the incarnationism of the canonical literature, Knox also sees two boundaries: (a) the Fourth Gospel as representing the limit to which docetism is taken and (b) either Hebrews or the Pauline letters as representing the limit to which kenoticism is taken.[4]

Knox's contentions will not by any means convince everyone. They are certainly not without technical difficulties, and as a trained biblical scholar he is, of course, not unaware of these. Yet neither are they without persuasive-

---

[2] John Knox, *The Humanity and Divinity of Christ* (Cambridge: Cambridge University Press, 1967), pp. 12ff.

[3] Knox, *Humanity and Divinity*, p. 14.

[4] Ibid., p. 19.

ness. Every literary historian knows well the difficulty of getting behind any highly developed and influential theory to states of mind that antedate it. The difficulty is in some respects similar to that of the anthropologist who, in trying to understand the thought of a primitive people, must try to get behind deeply ingrained processes of logical reasoning to a thought-process that is neither logical nor illogical but simply alogical. There are notorious pitfalls. The cavalier attempts of some of our recent forefathers to find, behind traditional understandings of Jesus, an exemplar of modern politico-religious ideologies, have made scholars abnormally cautious in applauding such ventures. As long ago as 1937, Henry J. Cadbury called attention to such pitfalls in his highly perceptive study, *The Peril of Modernizing Jesus*, whose very title embodies what Krister Stendahl has called "one of the most important insights of biblical studies in the 20th century." [5] Knox's proposals, whatever their merits, certainly do not modernize biblical thought in the way Cadbury pilloried.

Whether Knox is right or not, there is no doubt that both docetic and kenotic tendencies reappeared in the Middle Ages, which lacked our access to the background of the New Testament documents. The crypto-monophysite tendencies to which I have already referred attest a much more extreme form of kenoticism than any that could have commended themselves either to Paul or to the writer of the letter to the Hebrews. Crypto-docetism was also prevalent in the Middle Ages. In the museum of the Flemish abbey of Tongerlo, near Antwerp, is a piece of a reredos, said to be fifteenth-century English, depicting God the Father in the conventional manner as a bearded man. In his extended hand is the Dove in whose beak is the Host, which the Dove is depositing in the lap of the Virgin. The piece is presumed

[5] Krister Stendahl, in Wayne A. Meeks (ed.), *The Writings of St. Paul* (New York: W. W. Norton & Company, 1972), p. 422.

to have been cut out as heretical. It exemplifies, at any rate, the extreme forms to which docetism could sometimes be taken in the late Middle Ages.

Not till the nineteenth century was there the beginning of a break in the rigorous mould of traditional Christian theology in the West.[6] It happened to appear in a distinctly dogmatic context. In some Lutheran circles was developed a special version of the theory known as *communicatio idiomatum, antidosis tōn idiōmatōn.* It appeared as a heterodox understanding of the doctrine propounded by Cyril of Alexandria and other Greek Fathers that notwithstanding the separation of the human and divine natures in Christ, the attributes of the one might be predicated of the other. In the mid-nineteenth century, Thomasius of Erlangen, a Lutheran theologian, propounded the theory that the Incarnation could be understood as a self-emptying of God. On this view, God was indeed in Christ as Paul proclaimed; nevertheless, for the special occasion, God had emptied himself of his attributes so that Jesus, lacking the divine omniscience and omnipotence, had been under the same limitations as other men. That made him fully human without denying the central Christian doctrine of the Incarnation.

This view might have met even more resistance than it did among Lutherans had not it happened to commend itself to their theologians for a dogmatic reason. They were disposed to be hospitable to any theological notion that seemed anti-Calvinistic, for traditionally Lutherans accused Calvinists of artificially gluing the two natures of Christ together like two boards. The view proposed by Thomasius and others came to be known as kenotic theory. It appeared

---

[6] A comprehensive account of the history of christological kenoticism was provided by A. B. Bruce, *The Humiliation of Christ* (New York: Hodder and Stoughton, 1876). Cf. Paul Henry, S.J., in *Dictionnaire de la Bible, Supplément,* ed. L. Pirot, 1928ff, x (1950), cols. 1–161, s.v. "Kénose," which has a good bibliography.

later in the century in a more modified form among Anglican theologians such as Charles Gore.

The theory provided an answer to the stock questions people asked of the champions of Chalcedonian orthodoxy, Catholic or Reformed. For instance, if Christ was both "fully man" and "fully God," did he possess the divine attributes of omniscience and omnipotence as a baby on his mother's knee and as a prisoner on the way to his shameful death? The testimony of the Gospels seemed against such a claim. Moreover, the text in Philippians[7] seemed clearly to support the view that in some miraculous way he divested himself *(heauton ekenōse)* of the attributes of divinity for the singular purpose of the Incarnation.

Such adventurous theologians generally failed to convince the traditionalists of their day, and the reason for their failure is peculiarly relevant to our present enterprise. These traditionalists attached immense importance to the classic Christian notion of God as the Sovereign Lord standing over and beyond his creation. Typical of the objections from the theological establishment of the day was that of William Temple: "What was happening to the rest of the universe," asked that great archbishop, "during the period of our Lord's earthly life? To say that the Infant Jesus was from His cradle exercising providential care over it all is certainly monstrous; but to deny this, and yet to say that the Creative Word was so self-emptied as to have no being in the Infant Jesus is to assert that for a certain period the history of the world was let loose from the control of the Creative Word." [8] If Temple's question sounds crude to modern ears, let them listen also to the comments of his Scottish Presbyterian contemporary, Donald Baillie, who writes that

---

[7] Phil. 2:7.

[8] W. Temple, *Christus Veritas* (London: Macmillan, 1962), pp. 142f. Referring to kenotic christology as presented by H. R. Mackintosh, Temple called the difficulties "intolerable" (p. 142).

the objection "that the question presupposes a crude and false separation of the Persons of the Trinity from each other" is vain, for the crude separation is in the kenotic theory that Temple was criticizing, so that if Temple's question sounds crude, the crudity "derives directly from the theory which it is intended to criticize, since his method is that of *reductio ad absurdum*." [9]

That two such perspicacious and tolerant churchmen as William Temple and Donald Baillie should be so unsympathetic to even the restrained forms that kenoticism had been taking in their day seems remarkable only if we allow ourselves to forget how astonishingly literalistic even the most philosophically-minded churchmen in the West could be a few generations ago on any subject that seemed to threaten their very latinized understanding of Chalcedonian orthodoxy. Only those as openminded as Donald Baillie could have gone on to admit, as he did, that the use made of the kenotic idea by Russian Orthodox theologians like Bulgakov[10] and Gorodetzky deserved more immunity from attack. What Baillie found unacceptable, he tells us, was the particular use the so-called "liberal" theologians of the day were making of kenotic theory in their christology, not the use to which Russians were putting it, namely, "as indicating something which is involved in Creation itself and even in the Trinity." [11]

That brings us to the nub of the question raised in our preliminary glance at the way in which kenotic theory

[9] D. M. Baillie, *God Was in Christ* (New York: Charles Scribner's Sons, 1948), p. 96.

Modern kenotic christologies have been severely criticized by many. See, e.g., F. J. Hall, *The Kenotic Theory* (London: Longmans Green, 1898), and, among contemporary theologians, E. R. Fairweather, "The 'Kenotic' Christology" in F. W. Beare, *The Epistle to the Philippians* (London: A. & C. Black, 1959), pp. 159–174.

[10] See his *Du Verbe incarné*. (Paris: Aubier, 1943), where he suggests that the creative act is kenotic.

[11] Baillie, *God Was in Christ*, p. 98.

developed in the nineteenth century and suggests a clue for the case for which I intend to argue. At first sight, Donald Baillie's resistance to the modest use to which Gore had put the theory in a limited christological context, coupled with Baillie's comparative friendliness toward Bulgakov's much more encompassing use of it, seems paradoxical. The paradox vanishes when we find *why* Baillie, like many theologians of his time, suspected kenotic solutions to christological puzzles, yet was more perceptive than most in seeing that his strictures need not apply to kenoticism in the more radical form of a larger theological principle. The reason is plain. Kenoticism could be no solution of christological conundrums inherited from Nicaea and Chalcedon *unless* it could subsume such questions under a wider frame of theological reference. He did not by any means propose that it could; but he was admitting something such as one might suggest of, say, university administration: a proposed reform would seem to be unable to cure the ills of the Department of Physics or French; yet, if it could be shown to represent a principle so fundamental that it could, be successfully applied to the whole structure of the university, then, presumably, a fair-minded man would have to review the low opinion of it that he had formerly held.

That such theologians should have looked with so much hostility at the new kenotic answers to the old puzzles was due to their having adopted, however unconsciously, the rigid conceptual model that came out of the Latin theological heritage. The model might be sketched as follows. Behind or beyond the natural universe is God the Father, he who by definition acts and, by the same definition, cannot be acted upon. That means he cannot suffer, for *patior* ("to suffer") is a passive verb-form that *means* "to be acted upon." Not only is he *pantokratōr*, the ruler of all things; he is *par métier* the One on whom the universe depends for its very existence, without whose continual support Nature herself would be annihilated. According to this model the

Trinity provides the assurance that whatever outgoingness there be in God, he remains the ground of all Being, the solid and secure prop of all things. That he has also other functions, other faces, other *hypostases*, as expounded in the classic doctrine of the Trinity, cannot affect that essentially active and supportive character of divine Being. His sovereignty is understood as intrinsically incapable of diminishment or limitation. That, indeed, is what makes the Incarnation the glorious absurdity that the most penetrating geniuses in the history of Christian thought, from Tertullian to Kierkegaard, have delighted to call it. It is, according to this model, a surprise *par excellence*. It is not like anything even God would ever normally do. Yet he does it, so manifesting his infinite power to do even what seems metaphysically undoable. It is a case, beyond human expectation, of the exercise of the infinite power of God. As so often in traditional models, *omnipotens* is taken to mean not only the ability to do anything that does not deny the divine nature, but the habitual, unfettered and unrestrained use of that ability.

The model makes God seem somewhat like an oriental despot twenty feet tall, and of course I am far from suggesting that men of such deep spirituality as Donald Baillie and William Temple ever worshipped such a deity. Nevertheless, theologians sometimes build worse than they know; that is, they are sometimes so afraid of losing their conceptual models that they unconsciously cling to them even in the face of their own better judgment. H. R. Mackintosh and others of the same period were able to see that the models might have obscured and diminished the truth about divine Being more than ever they had clarified it. Chalcedon, though it drew attention to certain ways of thinking about Christ which, if pursued, could have emasculated Christian thought, might have become itself an impediment to the clarity of that thought and the vision of the plenitude of the Christian faith.

I shall argue that the traditional Christian understanding of the nature of God, by adherence to stultified modes of thought, has resulted, not least in the Western Church, in an inadequate grasp of the nature of divine Being. More specifically I shall try to show that if the dimension of Being that theologians call God is to be understood as creative of all that falls within the scope of the natural sciences, which of course is indisputably orthodox Jewish, Christian, and Muslim teaching, then the kenotic notion sheds more light on what the nature of God must be than do the more traditional theological formulations of these respective heritages. That is not to deny that the suspicions of those who, like Temple and Baillie, sensed something wrong with the particular form in which the kenotic theory was expressed in christological discussions may have been well founded. For if the kenotic theory ought to be applied to philosophical understanding of the nature of divine Being, the restriction of it to a narrow and dogmatic christological rescue operation would be more likely to distort than to express it.

We have already noted Simone Weil's proposal about the kenotic nature of divine creation. Remarking that divine creation could not be an act of self-expansion on the part of God but must be an act of restraint and renunciation, she proposed the view that God, in the act of creation, empties a part of his Being, accepting the diminution. From her special vantage-point, Jewish and unbaptized yet passionately in love with the Catholic Church, she even interprets the remark in the Apocalypse about the Lamb slain from the foundation of the world[12] as an affirmation about the self-emptying of God *in creation*. God, by permitting the existence of anything distinct from himself and "worth infinitely less than himself" denies himself; that is, creation

---

[12] Rev. 13:8. An ambiguity in the Greek makes her exegesis questionable; but that need not concern us here.

on God's part must always entail self-denial, self-emptying. She goes on:

> The religions which have a conception of this renunciation, this voluntary distance, this voluntary effacement of God, his apparent absence and his secret presence here below, these religions are true religion, the translation into different languages of the great Revelation. The religions which represent divinity as commanding wherever it has the power to do so are false. Even though they are monotheistic they are idolatrous.[13]

The implications of her view for Christian life and worship are far-reaching indeed. We cannot profitably go direct to God. We must first pass through his kenosis:

> If one goes to God directly, it is then Jehovah (or Allah). We have to *empty God of his divinity* in order to love him. He emptied himself of his divinity by becoming man, then of his humanity by becoming a corpse (bread and wine), matter. We must love God through and beyond our own joy, our own affliction, our own sins (past ones). We must love him through and beyond the joys, the afflictions, and the sins of other men—and without any consolation. To love God through and beyond a certain thing is to love that thing in purity; the two sentiments are identical.[14]

Her view also affects the notion of repentance and of compassion: "To love God through and beyond our sins is repentance. To love God through and beyond the affliction of others is compassion for our neighbor." [15] She provides an example in her characteristically breathtaking style: "A victim of misfortune is lying in the road, half dead with

---

[13] Simone Weil, *Waiting on God*, trans. E. Craufurd, (London: Collins, Fontana Books, 1959), p. 102.

[14] Simone Weil, *The Notebooks of Simone Weil*, 2 vols., trans. A. Wills (New York: G. P. Putnam's Sons, 1956), Vol. I, p. 283.

[15] Ibid.

hunger. God pities him but cannot send him bread. But I am here and luckily I am not God. I can give him a piece of bread. It is my one point of superiority over God." [16] Humiliation is so fundamental to Being that she even says: "If God had not been humiliated, in the person of Christ, he would be inferior to us." [17]

The metaphysical presuppositions underlying Simone Weil's affirmations here differ from those lying behind the conventional, traditional way of conceptualizing God in the West. Self-emptying is seen as belonging to the essential nature of God. His creativity is therefore of that essential nature, so that presumably, as in Origen, God is endlessly creating. The self-emptyingness of his creativity is also the model for human generosity and compassion, which are inseparable from each other as belonging to the creativity of genuine human love.[18] God, seen in such a light, may indeed be called omnipotent; but the power is not power as we commonly understand it in human affairs. God does not *wield* power *over* his creation; on the contrary, he exercises it in the creative act, and the exercise of it is the exercise of his love. So in God love and power might be shown to be identical, or at most two aspects of the same thing.

What becomes, then, of the notion of God as the ground of all Being? How can that which is forever engaged in self-emptying be the eternal and immutable ground? Once again, the traditional model has misled many into seeing God as primarily "the impermeable." As in Hegel, they have a God who may permit his creatures to pain one another, but who remains invulnerable to any such disturbance. It is then that the Incarnation becomes such an

---

[16] Simone Weil, *First and Last Notebooks*, trans. R. Rees (London: Oxford University Press, 1970), p. 297.

[17] Ibid., p. 97

[18] Weil, *Waiting on God*, p. 103. Her debt to the religious ideas of the Indus Valley will be obvious to all who are familiar with that heritage.

incomprehensible mystery, for it is seen as an exception to God's "ordinary" behavior, an exception that needs special theological pleading, special dogmatic revelation. The Hegelian God's invulnerability may have been indeed more than anything else what the genius of Kierkegaard detected as the radical falsehood in Hegel's type of rationalism. We are traditionally conditioned to seeing the self-emptying of God, the paining of God, as depriving God of all that assures his independence and guarantees his ontological dependability. A God who is affected by anything must be to that extent subject to something other than himself and is therefore no God but, rather, a fiction or, at most, an epiphenomenon that emerges in non-God.

Traditional Christian doctrine does of course provide a means of attributing to God the Christ-like qualities that Christians acclaim in the Gospels as divine. In doing so, Christians invoke the great mystery of their faith, the *mysterium Christi* by which they are enabled to say "God is love"; but such an affirmation remains unintelligible to orthodox Christians apart from the elaborate, not to say cumbersome, doctrine of the Trinity, which tries to preserve the notion of the Father as the immutable, impermeable ontological ground.

The attempt to safeguard the notion of God as immutable ground is nevertheless indispensable to any understanding of God that does not reduce divinity to an emergent epiphenomenon of the human spirit. The *malaise* many of us feel about the conventional formulations of Christian orthodoxy at this point is that they seem to suggest that since God is the ground of all Being he cannot be, *for that very reason*, the self-emptying One. If, however, we are to take seriously the idea of God the Creator, why should he be conceived only as the Almighty One who twirls the universe by the exercise of his infinite power? Why should not he be eternally creating it by the eternal self-emptyingness of his Being? Dante, who was able to express medieval insights in a poetic way far beyond the scope of the scholastic method of Saint Thomas, seems to have perceived in his own way the kenotic principle with which we are to be concerned. After describing in the *Paradiso* his awesome vision of the splendor of the Trinity, he concludes at length with his celebrated allusion to *l'amor che muove il sole e l'altre stelle*. Catholic devotion to the Sacred Heart, which was practiced by the Carthusians before the Jesuits took it up, no doubt appealed, however unconsciously, to the same principle. The more modern popular development of that devotion, stimulated by the visions of Margaret Mary Alacoque has been unfortunately associated with a garish iconography that has deflected the attention of many from the profound significance of the underlying principle.

That principle is: no theology can even begin to provide a plausible philosophical answer to the celebrated question of Leibniz that Heidegger has repeated, "Why is there anything at all and not just nothing?" until it recognizes that if there be a God at all who can be invoked by way of answer to that most philosophical of all questions, he must be a God whose very nature it is to be self-emptying in the exercise of his creative Being. Creation, on this view, must therefore be the eternal process that Origen envisioned. This does not mean that God is compelled to create, any more than either the Bible or Saint Thomas means that God is compelled to be merciful. It means that the power of God cannot be other than the power of his creative love. Only by recognizing that love conquers all *(omnia vincit amor)*[19] does the saying of the Johannine letter become intelligible: *ho theos agapē esti*,[20] God is love.

[19] Vergil, *Eclogues*, 10, 69.
[20] 1 John 4:16.

CHAPTER V

Kenoticist Difficulties Provide the Clue

Well spake he who said that the un-measurable Father was himself sub-jected to measure in the Son; for the Son is the measure of the Father, since he also comprehends him.

—Irenaeus (second century),
Adversus omnes haereses,
4, 4, 2.

MOST of us have largely forgotten the twenty-year *floreat* of kenoticism in British theology. In that brief period, extending through the last decade of the nineteenth century and the first decade of our own, it had a vogue in England such as the *Religionsgeschichtlicheschule* was having in Germany about the same time, such as Barth was to have in Scotland in the forties, and the so-called death-of-God theology in the United States in the sixties. As in other cases, not all who talked the theological idiom of the day knew what they were talking about. As William Bright wrote impatiently at the time: "This kenotic theory is taken up by many almost as *pax vobiscum* was by a personage in Ivanhoe." [1]

Kenotic theories, after fascinating theologians for a time, and even exerting considerable influence on the thinking of some of them, soon became widely suspect and have remained largely out of vogue today. The First World War may have finished off whatever interest had remained at the time of its outbreak in 1914, for wars can be as damaging to thought as they are destructive of life. At any rate, he who seeks to vindicate kenoticism today and to rehabilitate it in a new and radical form is assured of at least one advantage: he cannot be charged with pandering to theological fashion. Vincent Taylor, though personally sympathetic to it, was so sensitive to its disrepute in theological controversies that in a work containing one of the best accounts of the history of criticism of it[2] he remarks that theologians are tempted to avoid the word kenosis "and speak rather of self-limitation." [3] Why should a type of theory that is *prima facie* both appealing and profound have fallen so much out of favor and even into oblivion? I wish to argue that what many theologians have feared is not kenoticism itself but, rather, what it might do to upset cherished trinitarian models that they took to be the bulwarks of Christian orthodoxy. I hope that will clear the way for proposing the more radical form of the theory that I defend.

Kenoticism seemed even to the most sympathetic to diminish either the humanity or the divinity of Christ. Frank Weston was among those who felt it diminished his humanity, while in Germany a few decades earlier Ritschl had complained that in kenoticism "Christ, at least in His

[1] B. J. Kidd (ed.), *Selected Letters of William Bright*, as quoted in A. M. Ramsey, *An Era in Anglican Theology: From Gore to Temple* (New York: Charles Scribner's Sons, 1960), p. 36.

[2] Vincent Taylor, *The Person of Christ* (London: Macmillan and Company, Ltd., 1958), Chapter XIX, "Christology and the Kenosis."

[3] Ibid., p. 270f.

earthly existence, has no Godhead at all." [4] It is remarkable, indeed, that Ritschl, who taught that the divinity of Christ should be taken not as an historical statement of fact but as an expression of his "revelational value" *(Offenbarungswert)* for the community that trusts in him as God, should feel that kenoticism makes it impossible for God to be found in Jesus.

Of the three principal objections that Vincent Taylor thinks must be taken into account, perhaps the most curious is that it is "mythological." Yet that objection, he assures us, "is felt by many to be strong." [5] Why so? As Rudolf Bultmann has abundantly reminded us, the New Testament writers used many mythological notions that depended on now outmoded cosmology, such as that of a three-tiered universe. Much more importantly, we must not at any point forget that *mythoi* are indispensable to all religion. God, if known at all, must be known under human symbols. Pascal's seventeenth-century proposal to think of him as a point moving at infinite speed may titillate the minds of those who are just being weaned from the bearded-man symbol; but like all symbols for God it is anthropomorphic too. Symbols may be literally in the shape of a man; but even Pascal's is in the "shape" of human geometry.

Since every significant religious idea in human history has had to be mythologically expressed, why boggle at a mythological element in kenoticism? Consider only, for example, the eternal begetting of the Son, the coming down from heaven, the sitting at the right hand of the Father, the Spirit descending in tongues of fire and settling upon each of the apostles. Surely we were never meant to suppose that the Son of God came down from the sky or has gone thither

[4] Albrecht Ritschl, *Justification and Reconciliation* (English translation of *Die christliche Lehre von der Rechtfertigung und Versöhnung*, 3 vols., 1870–74), p. 410.

[5] Taylor, *Person of Christ*, p. 299.

to sit on a throne adjacent to his Father's. Why should the presence of mythological elements in kenotic theory be accounted so strong an objection to it? The real difficulty would seem to lie elsewhere, and I hope to show that it does.

Donald Baillie, who was among the objectors, thought of kenoticism as implying that God was temporarily turned into man, exchanging his divinity for humanity.[6] It seems that he had in mind the cruder stories of metamorphosis in classical Greek lore; for instance, the action of Zeus, who, when he fell in love with Leda, a mortal princess, turned himself into a swan in order to seduce her, which seduction, duly accomplished, resulted in the birth of the Dioscuri, half gods, half mortals. If so, Baillie would have been horrified, of course, at even the slightest *soupçon* of resemblance he might have suspected. Not even the boldest of the German kenoticists give any ground, however, for such suspicion. J. A. Ebrard, in his *Dogmatik*, published in 1851, had expressly insisted that the incarnate Word did not lose his divinity. Nor could one find ground for the suspicion in Thomasius or Dorner or Biedermann.[7] Even W. F. Gess, for all the extravagance of some of his utterances warrants no such suspicion. Certainly nothing could have been more remote from the mind of Gore or Mackintosh or Forsyth than the notion Baillie seems to have feared. The great exponents of kenoticism in the nineteenth and early twentieth centuries were attracted to it because, while it seemed a possible way out of some of the more intractable traditional difficulties bequeathed by Nicaea and Chalcedon, it did better justice to what the New Testament documents report. I would suggest that it also exhibits the all-important

[6] D. M. Baillie, *God Was in Christ* (New York: Charles Scribner's Sons, 1948), p. 96.

[7] Cf. Claude Welch (ed.), *God and Incarnation in Mid-Nineteenth Century German Theology* (New York: Oxford University Press, 1965).

notion to which I have alluded earlier: by putting self-limitation at the heart of God it exalts humility as an implicate
of the divine love, which is surely a notion that pre-
eminently accords with biblical testimony about God.

The objections arise because kenoticism has been developed within a dogmatic context in which its champions
have had to face the impossible task of reconciling it with
the array of theological propositions that arise out of a
complex traditional trinitarian structure. Paradoxically, that
very structure that was designed to safeguard the Christian
mode of conceptualizing God has ended by raising obstacles
against and arousing suspicions about almost any creative
theological idea that might conceivably be proposed by way
of articulating the faith of the Church, even one that may
have antedated, as we have seen, the more complex
development of the trinitarian model. Here then is at least
one reason for the reluctance of some of the most sensitive
kenoticists to specify as clearly as might have been expected
of them how the kenosis may be supposed to work.

Gore was among those who wisely advocated agnosticism
about the details of the kenotic operation. Those who felt
obliged to be more explicit resorted to strangely ingenious
proposals: Frédéric Louis Godet, for instance, suggested
that the cosmic functions of the Son were taken over by the
Father and the Spirit, as though the Persons of the Trinity
arranged to look after the administration of the universe
during the absence of one of their number, as partners in a
law firm arrange to take care of things when one of them
goes on vacation. Godet was an eminent Swiss Protestant
scholar who, after being tutor to the Crown Prince Friedrich Wilhelm of Prussia, became professor in his native
Neuchâtel, also helping to found the theological faculty of
the Free Church there. That such a man should have felt
the need to resort to such a bizarre proposal is eloquent. It
exemplifies both the attractiveness of kenotic theory and the
extreme need that was felt among responsible theologians to

uphold trinitarian doctrine even if doing so involved them in the crassest literalism.

In the thought of that day the relation of the kenosis to the consciousness of Jesus assumed considerable importance. Perhaps the most thoroughgoing and certainly a very circumspect treatment was provided by Frank Weston. He wrote of the Christ of the Gospels as "the Son of God self-restrained in conditions of manhood." He suggested that the Son imposed upon himself a law requiring him to "taste of the unconsciousness . . . of the unborn child." Yet he boldly criticized Clement of Alexandria and other ancient Fathers for obscuring the manhood of Christ, and he particularly objected to the notion of a "self-abandoned Logos," which he thought a diminishment of the human nature of Christ. Weston also felt, however, that the general thrust of New Testament teaching was toward the notion of the permanence, during Christ's earthly life, "of the universal life and cosmic function of the eternal Word." [8]

Many critics protested against the notion of Christ's gradual awakening to, or intermittent awareness of, his divinity. Here is a characteristic expression of what such critics found offensive: "It can only have been in mature manhood and perhaps intermittently that Christ became aware of His divinity—which must have remained an object of *faith* to the very end . . . In any case, it is only by degrees that the full meaning of His relationship to the Father, with its eternal implicates, can have broken on Jesus' mind." [9]

Consider how an average, educated person, not particularly committed to Christianity or any other religion, would react to such a suggestion. At first sight it would seem to such a person fairly unremarkable, even granting that Christ

[8] Welch (ed.), *God and Incarnation*, p. 115.
[9] H. R. Mackintosh, *The Doctrine of the Person of Jesus Christ* (Edinburgh: T. and T. Clark, 1912), p. 418.

is to be understood as in some way divine. A man may have a sense of destiny or divine commission yet not have it always in full intensity. At first he is groping uneasily, while gradually the realization breaks in upon him that he is no ordinary man, no man with an ordinary mission. Yet he is not sure. As his life unfolds, however, he sees the pieces fall into place. From time to time he is suddenly aware that his *is* an extraordinary mission and destiny. Nevertheless, the unfolding does not proceed in orderly, regular fashion, as in the rolling out of a map. The man is sometimes discouraged or exhausted. Is it not so with every human awareness? Even the man who is most happy in his work is not happy at it all the time. Sometimes he loses heart; sometimes he questions whether, after all, he has chosen the right profession. But then, as his kindly friends tell him, things will look better in the morning; and so they do. At last, when he enters into the twilight of his life, he feels more and more satisfied that he has fulfilled his mission. Why not, then, say something similar of the life of Christ? Be it the greatest mission that ever was, might not the same principle apply? The infant Jesus gradually becomes aware of his uniqueness. So already at the age of twelve he is astonishing the learned rabbis. At last, a mature young man, he sets forth on his public ministry, increasingly conscious of who he is and what he must do. Yet even on the eve of the Passion he is hesitant, and in the cry of dereliction on the Cross he seems utterly crushed by that agony of doubt that is a familiar moment of our human condition and without which we could hardly call him human at all.

There seems little wrong with all that till we try to square it with the Nicene and Chalcedonian formulations. As soon as we try to do so, we see that it *entails* the notion of the self-abandonment of the divine attributes. That brings us to the nub of the problem. The objection that was most recurrent in the critical literature and was generally accounted the most fundamental is against the notion of the self-abandonment of the divine attributes. Wherever this element in kenoticism seemed minimized, to that extent the strictures were less severe. The forms of the theory that made prominent the notion of self-abandonment were those that alarmed even the sympathetic and brought all kenotic theories under a cloud.

No writer on kenoticism is more perceptive than H. R. Mackintosh, and nowhere does he come so near what I think is the heart of the matter as when he examines what happens when the discussion comes to center upon "the idea of divine immutability." He suggests that "what Christ reveals in God is rather the infinite mobility of absolute grace. . . . What is immutable in God is the holy love which makes His essence. . . . This self-renouncing, self-retracting act . . . is no negation of His nature; it is the opposite, it is the last assertion of His nature as love." [10] A more recent writer remarks: "From all eternity there has been, so to speak, the Christness in God, which is to say that God's essential nature is creative love. . . ." [11]

The trinitarian structure of the Christian doctrine of God, however, dogs the footsteps of all who try to make such notions square with the traditional model. Modern writers bent on trying to interpret it to their contemporaries in such a way as to make sense of the divine attributes have sometimes gone to ridiculous extremes only to end up with a feeble version of an old textbook heresy. Henry Pitney Van Dusen, for instance, while President of Union Theological Seminary, New York City, actually proposed the analogy of Theodore Roosevelt as having three different "modes of operation." First, there was the public figure, the President of the United States; second, there was the explorer, the hunter, the leader of his Rough Riders; and third there was

[10] Ibid., p. 472f.

[11] W. R. Bowie, *Jesus and the Trinity* (Nashville, Tenn.: Abingdon Press, 1960), p. 89.

the jovial father with whom his children played at home.[12]
Whatever other effects such a proposal may have, it must
surely be accounted unoriginal, since almost any theological
seminary middler could identify it as what was said by
Sabellius and other modalists more than seventeen centuries
before Van Dusen was proposing it as a sop for the modern
mind. Its unsatisfactoriness had been sufficiently demonstrated even before the triumph of Nicaea. Leonard Hodgson's interpretation goes so much in the opposite direction
that Gustav Aulén accounted it close to tritheism.[13] Both
tendencies traduce what the Church has struggled to say in
the trinitarian formulae, and neither does anything to
mitigate the difficulties the trinitarian formulae present for
kenotic theory.

The interpretations I have just mentioned not only
misrepresent what the Fathers of Nicaea and Chalcedon
intended; they do nothing to elucidate the way in which the
divine attributes are to be related. Such interpretations
would not have fitted the mould of the thought of the
keenest minds of the fourth and fifth centuries. Paramount
in their conceptualization of any divine attribute was its
supportive function. By that I mean that they believed the
supreme value of omniscience as of every other attribute lay
in its providing support for the universe. If these attributes
were absent or even in any way quiescent, God would be
undependable. He would be of no more value than would
any one of the gods in a pagan pantheon.

One could not usefully pray, for instance, to a divine
Being whose omnipotence was in any way capable of being
abandoned, for to the extent that he abandoned it he might
not be able to help; nor could one confidently pray to a God

[12] H. P. Van Dusen, *Spirit, Son and Father* (New York: Charles Scribner's Sons,
1958), p. 174.
[13] See, e.g., L. Hodgson, *The Doctrine of the Trinity* (New York: Charles
Scribner's Sons, 1944), pp. 85ff.

who could in any way set aside his omniscience, for then he might lack knowledge at the very point at which he needed it to help; and least of all would one be content with a God who could be occasionally bereft of his omnipresence, for then, when most needed, he might not be there. We might well ask also: if one set of attributes can be laid aside, why not another? Suppose, then, that God could lay aside what have sometimes been called "moral" attributes, such as justice, mercy, and love? What if we pled for divine mercy only to be told that we were out of luck, since it happened that God had laid his mercy aside this month, so that we were left only with his justice? Or, again, what if we cried out at monstrous cruelty only to be told that the divine justice was temporarily in abeyance? God would have become no better than a constituent of a pagan pantheon.

There, indeed, the root of the trouble begins to show. For polytheism was far closer to the men of the age in which the Nicene and Chalcedonian formulae were produced than it could possibly be for us. For us it is intellectually too remote to be a live option. We merely smile at the old tales and sagas of the gods. Pantheism or naturalism might well seduce a twentieth-century Jew or Christian from his faith; polytheism never. True, it had lost its hold on educated people by Augustine's day; nevertheless, it was still a possible way of thinking; it was still part of the climate of thought. Christianity offered nothing if it did not offer release from the sense of being at the mercy of capricious gods and demons. So whatever was attributed to the Christian God must be such as to assure his total reliability. This great insight finds characteristic expression in the Epistle of James: with God "is no variableness, neither shadow of turning." [14]

Now we ought to be very careful here to recognize how important it was for the Christians of that age to make the

[14] James 1:17.

point we have just noticed. In so doing, they were right on their target. Though the primitive mind that deals in gods and goddesses, in witches and fairies, in demons and goblins, in elves and gnomes and other sprites, is already awakened to the religious dimension of life, it is still at the mythopoeic stage. Incapable of metaphysical or indeed of any abstract thought, its great need is to be taught that whatever the God-dimension is, it lies beyond such picturesque fancies and conceits. A new *kind* of symbol is becoming necessary to replace the symbols of primitive folklore. To bring into focus the radical difference between the new kind of symbol and the old, the first thing to be said is that God, whoever or whatever God is, provides support for all that is not-God. The discovery of that supportive function affords the greatest joy humanity has at that point so far experienced.

There have been few discoveries of that magnitude or importance. One had been the discovery of the power of the human mind to turn inwards and find a new world, a new dimension of being, a new realm of energy and power. Another was the discovery of what abstract reasoning power could accomplish. Now came the recognition that the source of that energy and power lay beyond even that inner realm of the human mind. So Augustine, when he turned introspectively into his mind, found "above" it *(supra mentem)* the incommunicable light that he recognized as the source of that mind. Such discoveries are intoxicating. When primitive man comes to an awareness that beyond the senses lies a spiritual world, he proclaims in no uncertain terms the value of his discovery. He is extremely jealous lest anyone say or do anything to detract attention from it, for that would be to put the clock back. So with all such discoveries. When to the discovery that finds expression in monotheism is attached the disclosure of the notion that the Eternal has entered into time "for us men and for our salvation," the importance of the supportive function reaches its zenith.

Our situation today, however, is considerably different. We need to penetrate beyond the models that were so skilfully constructed for those for whom that supportive function was so peculiarly important. The exponents of the kenotic theory, especially the earlier ones such as Thomasius, erred in trying to expound kenoticism without reviewing the conceptual models that not only envisaged immutability as the attribute *par excellence* but built into it a primitive cosmology that seemed to demand a correspondingly crude metaphysical understanding of immutability. That affected also their understanding of even the so-called "moral" attributes of God: justice seems more immutable than mercy, so men thought that while God might withdraw his mercy at pleasure, even God could not withdraw his own justice. To do so would be to diminish or in some way vitiate his immutability, which would be to wreck his "essential nature."

So readily was it assumed that God, being immutable, is impassible (that is, incapable of suffering), that till about the turn of the present century almost nobody seriously undertook even the defense of that proposition. It was taken to be axiomatic. When the Church of England's Archbishops' Doctrinal Commission, in September 1924, commissioned a study of the history of the doctrine of impassibility and an account of the influences that seemed to be bringing about a reaction against it in some quarters, J. K. Mozley, the author of that study, reported that his investigations revealed only two monographs specifically devoted to the subject.[15] One of these was in the third century: Gregory Thaumaturgus, *De passibili et impassibili in Deo*. The other was published in the year 1900: Marshall Randles, *The Blessed God. Impassibility*. This latter book defended the traditional

---

[15] J. K. Mozley, *The Impassibility of God* (Cambridge: Cambridge University Press, 1926).

doctrine against contrary opinions that were being voiced in his day. Nevertheless, such was the climate of thought by the late nineteenth century, at least in *avant-garde* circles of theological discussion, that the whole question was being obliquely raised in many ways even when it was not being specifically considered. Douglas White, for example, had argued from the costliness of forgiveness to the passibility of God in *Forgiveness and Suffering* published in 1913. We have already noticed that the previous year, H. R. Mackintosh had discussed kenotic views of his day critically but with many illuminating insights into the notion that self-abnegation belongs to God's creative act, so bringing under scrutiny the whole question of the divine impassibility. In 1914 Streeter also published an important paper on the subject.[16] By 1926 C. A. Dinsmore could say categorically, in *Atonement in Literature and Life*, that "there was a cross in the heart of God before there was one planted on the green hill outside of Jerusalem." Nevertheless, he insisted that God abides "in perfect felicity."

Father Thornton somewhat peremptorily disposed of the whole kenotic question in a few lines, on the ground that the exponents of kenotic theories had tried to deal with the problem "on too narrow a basis." He was in a sense right. We must ask, however, in what the narrowness consisted. He thought these exponents had been too "crudely external in their treatment of the divine attributes." [17] The trouble lay, however, deeper still, in their adherence to an unexamined understanding of immutability.

When theologians began to suggest that the justice and mercy of God are not separate attributes that must sometimes seem in conflict, they were moving in the right direction. In coming to see that the justice of God *is* his

---

[16] See Chapter VII.

[17] L. S. Thornton, *The Incarnate Lord* (London: Longmans, 1928), p. 262.

mercy and his mercy his justice, as certainly did John Baillie, for instance, they were nearing a vision of what must be done with the whole structure of Nicene and Chalcedonian formulations. As the justice of God must be so far beyond even the best of human justice as to comprehend also the divine mercy, so the mercy of God must be so far beyond the finest human mercy as to encompass the divine justice. In like manner the immutability of God must so far surpass any immutability we know in man or Nature as to encompass the divine love, and the divine love must so excel even the most sacrificial human love as to embrace what has been called the immutability of God. The immutability *is* the love, the love the immutability. So also with the omnipotence, omniscience, and omnipresence of God: they are not at all to be accounted an infinite degree of human power and wisdom and presence. If God is as worshipful as Christians have always claimed, these attributes must be so far beyond their human analogues as to be fused together, if one may so speak, with all possible divine attributes in the Being of God, which as classical Christian thought has perceived must be perfectly "simple." The simplicity need not consist, however, in the impassibility of divine Being. It might consist in the simplicity of love, which is simple in needing no attributes other than itself.

While no one would suppose that by divine omniscience is to be understood a mind stocked like a well-programmed computer, many have tended to think of God as "knowing everything" in the sense of possessing such knowledge as would enable him to score 100% in any examination that could be set. That is surely far too low a category in which to think of any divine attribute, for every attribute must be touched and illumined by the rest. Profound indeed, then, is the insight in Mackintosh's observation, already quoted, that what is immutable in God is the holy love that constitutes his essence. Yet we must understand that to talk of the divine love without the other attributes is to rob it of its character. Once again, only by a refined form of anthropomorphism can one talk of divine attributes as though they were gifts or talents, as we might say of an exemplary man that he was a great scholar and also a wonderful father, a good golfer and a fine musician too, both a linguist and a mathematician, and so forth. One can make such an inventory of a man's virtues and vices, deficiencies and talents, almost as one lists the holdings of a library or takes inventory of a grocery store. One could take away, say, the golfing prowess without affecting the rest. Or I might tell you of someone else who answers exactly to the above description except that he is tone-deaf, but is, on the other hand a chess master. It would be hardly different from my reporting that the one store carries exactly the same stock as the other except that the one has carrots but no beans, while the other has beans but lacks carrots. Logically, the human attributes are functioning as qualifiers in the same way as "bean-stocking" and "carrot-stocking" are qualifiers of "store."

Even the most finely honed logical tools cannot take us far, however, toward any knowledge of God we may feel disposed to claim. However we conceptualize the divine attributes, we find that they are, after all, at most only human symbols, devices for somehow trying to specify the "essential nature" of God. We can never be careful enough to avoid our tendency to see them as qualities that are, so to say, detachable and assessable in terms of a calculus of values. We have had abundant opportunity to see that today the doctrine of the Trinity may be more capable of aggravating that tendency than of mitigating it. Trinitarian doctrine is, of course, closely allied to that of the Incarnation, and it is out of this incarnational doctrine that the kenotic insight emerges. As soon as that insight is confronted by the trintarian model, however, it collapses. Attempts to fit it into that kind of pattern produce more nonsense than sense. Yet I believe the kenotic insight is perhaps the most profound and useful in the history of Christian thought and by far the most promising for its future. At least we should explore what happens when it is both loosed from the traditional trinitarian mould and placed in a wider frame of reference than the christological one whence it has issued and with which it has been so much associated. I propose, therefore, that we next address ourselves to that liberating enterprise.

CHAPTER VI

Creativity as Kenotic Act

On God's part creation is not an act of self-expansion but of restraint and renunciation.

—Simone Weil, Attente de Dieu

W E have seen how historical circumstances operated against a recognition of the kenotic nature of divine Being. There is, however, another powerful obstacle in our own common presuppositions. Before going further I should like to make some observations on this built-in obstacle to acceptance of the model I would commend. The obstacle arises from the natural human tendency to belittle or distort the nature of creativity.

Creative ability is by any reckoning rare. Most people, even among those endowed with outstanding natural gifts of memory, intelligence, and wit, are uncreative. They are sometimes properly described as competent, able, even brilliant. They may be useful and therefore valuable contributors to society and to the professions to which they belong. They may even be inventive and resourceful. Their inventiveness and resourcefulness consist, however, in their rearrangement of the same building blocks that have been already in use. They may be said to break new ground; but if so the ground they break is ground already known and waiting only to be tilled. Between all such activities and the authentic creation of novelty yawns an infinite chasm. No doubt similar reflections inspired the whimsical observation: most people think seldom, perhaps once in a lifetime; clever people somewhat oftener, say once in ten years; great philosophers oftener still, perhaps even every six months.

Popular misunderstanding of the nature of scientific progress also exhibits the point I would make here. Most people tend to think of science as an activity that is moving steadily on and even steadily gaining momentum in geometrical progression, as inevitably as a freewheeling bicycle gains momentum in descending a steep hill. In fact, the situation is very different. As every historian of science knows, the failures are numerous, the successes rare. Among a thousand hypotheses, not one may fit. The successes are achieved only when to the industry demanded of every working scientist are added those special qualities that are needed for scientific discovery: the imagination to conceive unlikely hypotheses, the "nose" for the right one, the openness to entertain it, and the courage to do so in face of the ridicule of colleagues and the impatience even of friends. From the standpoint of the current fashions of thought, the greatest scientific advances are generally along very unexpected lines. Great is the self-sacrifice their achievement entails, for the whole enterprise runs counter to what everyone has been "thinking" and "doing." It is a new birth.

When we think of mental activity and moral power we tend to think of the kind of activity and the kind of power that are to be found in competent copyists and able administrators, in skilful anthologists, in perceptive analysts. When we engage in such activity and exercise such power, we tire and grow weary. So we cry: "O that I had infinite strength! For then my power would not be so miserably restricted." Our concept of God, the *summum bonum,* reflects the model we are using. We think of God as having the infinite ability for self-expansion that we are conscious of lacking. The model we use, however grand its intellectual formulation, is a bricklayer's model. We say, in effect: "I am able to lay 700 bricks a day; star performers have been known to lay so many in an hour; if God were building he could lay an infinite number in an infinitesimal time." But brickbuilding, physical or mental, is not creative work. It provides a radically wrong kind of model for the creativity of God.

When people, whether Christian or otherwise, do their theologizing out of an experience of personal holiness they cannot easily fall into that kind of misunderstanding. For then their whole approach is changed. They say, rather: "The self-sacrifice it takes to bring into being the new relationship needed to make my marriage work, or the ingenuity needed to find my way into a new dimension of thought, or the patience required to let my son acquire his own strength, betokens resources at my command great enough to make such voluntary abdication of them possible for me. The renunciation of power implies that there is a reserve of power out of which the renunciation may be undertaken. If God exists, what, then, must be the divine resources that make possible the immense abdication of them that the creation, sustenance, and direction of the universe must demand?" We may conclude that such a reserve of power as God would need must be infinite; yet it is not to be infinitely used; it is to be abdicated for the creative purpose of God.

If the term "God" is to be intelligible, God must be sovereign and independent. If God be independent and sovereign, what use can there be for the exercise of that infinite reserve of power? Apart from any creative purposes in which he might choose to engage, there could be no conceivable occasion for him to exercise it. The situation would be very different indeed, if God could be self-seeking or ambitious. The biblical assurance that he is anything other than that would persuade only those who accept the biblical testimony as substantially true. But even if we set aside the Bible entirely, there is plainly no conceivable way in which God, being absolutely sovereign and independent, could possibly be ambitious or self-seeking. There is nothing for him to seek for himself, nothing toward which he could extend ambition, nothing for him to achieve, for *ex hypothesi* he is complete, perfect, self-subsistent. In choosing to engage in a creative purpose there is, so to speak, only one way for his power to go: it must be in some measure abdicated. It cannot go to a plus side, for there is no plus side to perfection; so if it is to go anywhere it must be to the minus side, that is, to the side of voluntary self-renunciation. God, in creating the universe, to that extent empties himself, letting the beings go free that he has created.

The effect of that state of affairs on the way in which the classical problem of evil has generally been treated and is still treated in contemporary philosophical circles by Professors Antony Flew and J. L. Mackie, for instance, should be abundantly evident to all who have the least familiarity with the way in which that problem is customarily approached by those contemporary philosophers who think the implications of theistic hypotheses worth examining. I intend to show in a later chapter how a kenotic understanding of the creative act clarifies the *unde malum* question and provides a solution to that thorniest of all problems that theists face.

If God is at all as I have proposed (and I would seek to maintain that in this respect my proposal is both metaphysically intelligible and consonant with biblical testimony), the act by which the universe is created entails an intrinsic sadness. That is what is proclaimed by those who say with Forsyth: "The cross was the reflection (or say rather the historic pole) of an act within Godhead." [1] The Incarnation

[1] P. T. Forsyth, *The Person and Place of Jesus Christ* (London: Independent Press, Ltd., 1909), p. 270.

remains, indeed, the supreme surprise, the proper occasion for the Church to sing her Christmas sequence: *Laetabundus exultet fidelis chorus*. For if we mortals are, because of the darkness of our unenlightened minds, as tragically separated from God as the Bible and the witness of the Church have always insisted, the revelation of the nature of God is bound to be surprising. Yet the cost of our redemption should not be the only occasion for our surprise. On the view I am proposing, that cost points to the even greater and more basic cost of bringing us into being. That is where the fundamental travail must lie. The Incarnation would be already entailed in the divine undertaking to bring our being about.

There are three other worthwhile possibilities to consider. Either (1) God is forced to work on a medium other than himself, which, despite the protestations of Brightman and other twentieth-century protagonists of that ancient view, implies a metaphysical dualism and therefore, in effect, two gods, that is, two insoluble mysteries rather than one; or (2) God, being sovereign and independent, wantonly spawns the universe, including the human race, which, having fallen, he then redeems by one peculiar act; or else (3) God and Nature are identical. I shall say something presently on the last of these alternatives. Meanwhile I would point out that both the first and the second render God less than even we mortals can conceive him to be. All our inquiry so far forces us to say that if God exists at all he must be at least One who in anguish voluntarily engages in self-sacrificial self-diminishment, abdicating his power in order to bring us into being.

Of the three alternatives I have listed, the only one that seems to merit serious inspection is the third, that is, the pantheistic thesis that God and Nature are to be identified. I shall therefore devote some time to it. Historians of religion tend to say that the early religious thought of some primitive peoples, notably the inhabitants of the Indus Valley, was pantheistic. That is, however, somewhat misleading. The Vedas, for instance, do not reflect a deliberate choice of this metaphysical standpoint over against another. They exhibit, rather, certain presuppositions that later writers, having become aware of viable alternatives, undertake to defend. The writers of that early religious literature are pantheists *faute de mieux*. They were so filled with awe and wonder at Being (a sense of wonder that has been widely lost by civilized people, to their immense impoverishment) that they did not have the same need as did later thinkers to distinguish dimensions of Being. They were as fascinated by the fact that breath comes into a new-born child, and that a dying man breathes his last, as by the fact that a man can imagine and remember and think.

When, however, Spinoza evolved his pantheistic system, he did indeed make a deliberate choice of it over against the traditional teaching of the synagogue. Spinoza could command widespread attention to, and interest in, his exposition of a pantheistic philosophy because he happened to live in the seventeenth century, after the great sixteenth-century renaissance of humanistic learning but before the development of modern science was fully under way. The proposal to identify God and Nature was singularly attractive to thoughtful people in the seventeenth and eighteenth centuries, and even throughout much of the nineteenth, because Nature was still to a great extent deified. She was still a goddess, invested with the symbolic accoutrements of divinity, rather than, as Nature now is taken to be, simply that which scientists are trying to understand. When even the lines between mental philosophy and natural philosophy (as the study of the natural sciences was called) were still ill defined, the proposal to coalesce Nature and God seemed not only attractive but an eminently fitting enterprise for an educated man, trained to the use of reason. The reduction of two mysteries to one could not but have seemed a welcome simplification. Spinoza's philosophical acumen has

continued to command the esteem of even those philosophers who dislike or distrust metaphysics. Stuart Hamp-
shire, no admirer of metaphysical enterprises, has given it a
nod of respect. That Spinoza fascinated not only his
contemporaries but many succeeding generations is unas-
tonishing.

Today the lines are differently drawn. Only poets deify
Nature, and many even among them seem to have given it
up. Naturalists as such no longer find any reason to do so. If,
then, anything is to be deified it must be a dimension of
Being beyond, though it need be by no means contrary to,
that dimension that scientists so successfully explore. In the
seventeenth century an intelligent and trained thinker
might properly propose *deus sive natura*, "God or Nature."
Today that option is open only to a neo-Gnostic Rip van
Winkle. Today our choice must be either: (1) to recognize
only that dimension of Being that is scientifically explorable
and therefore to exclude the concept of God as meaningless
or (as Professor van Buren has proposed) to call "God" a
marginal or "horizon" word, and so to rule out all rationale
for religious worship; or (2) to recognize, together with that
dimension of Being, another which, standing to it as a solid
geometry stands to plane, is that on which the natural
dimension depends. The pantheistic alternative is no longer
a live option. Spinoza would no more be a Spinozist today
than would Thomas be a Thomist.

Our whole understanding would be idle speculation, and
as remote from contemporary thought as are the Upanishads
and the Gathas, but for one inescapable fact of experience.
That inescapable fact is that when we human beings are
most fully self-aware we know very well that we are never
so fully ourselves as when we are creating. In creating we
are tempted to feel godlike (indeed among non-theists the
feeling may be uninhibited) because our activity is then
nearest to that of God; hence the danger of idolizing it.

Contemporary culture harbors a tendency that is the

outgrowth of a radically false presupposition. That presupposition makes the notion of creativity difficult for most people to understand. That is not to say it stifles creativity. Creativity is not so easily suffocated. That not even *nous* can inhibit *pneuma* was well recognized in biblical and classical Christian thought. The presupposition I have in mind is none the less highly injurious to our human condition and is at the root of many of our human ills, not least poverty and war. It has Lockian overtones, if not roots, for it inclines us to think of scientific advance and other human progress in terms of the appropriation of a hitherto existing but unknown territory, of the extraction of something from an established depository. On this view there are, so to say, so many marbles to be rolled in from an external *je ne sais quoi*. So we speak of, and sometimes provide funds for, scientific research, with the suggestion that a researcher's principal tool must always be, as the archaeologist's in fact is, a spade. From the notion of scientific research we proceed to what is taken to be an analogous academic pursuit, research in the humanities. Whatever may be accounted research, in the sense just indicated, is deemed respectable, for it always entails industry and sometimes produces useful results. It always requires a spade. In contrast to this solid and useful activity, creative enterprises are accounted fun, as though, letting the Muse take possession, one luxuriates in the outcome.

In all this there is indeed a dim recognition of an implicate of creative engagement, namely, the hard work that symbolizes the anguish of creativity that I am making so central to my theme. For such research uses the spade that commands an approval in contemporary intellectual circles on this side of the Iron Curtain comparable to the veneration that the hammer and sickle are supposed to evoke on the other. Nevertheless, all these symbols reflect a mistaken notion of how human achievements have brought about human progress and of what is its nature. True, we do sometimes hear of creative scholarship; but it is generally accounted either a hybrid or something of a fake, a name given to activities that look scholarly but cannot strictly speaking be so called since they are not performed with the approved tool. Only very rich institutions can afford such questionable activities, and then only in very limited numbers, since they are reckoned with champagne and caviar. On the contrary, but for our prejudices they would seem to be what indeed they are: bread and butter.

That so much of what has passed for scholarly research is now being done by computers has not yet by any means wholly succeeded in calling to our attention the radical falsity of our common presuppositions. We must hope that at length we shall see that human progress is attained only by evoking what has not before been there. Only through such creative activities is it possible for us to grasp who we are and what is our engagement with Being.

By and large, whatever domain of intellectual or cultural activity we care to inspect, we shall find in it vast non-creative deserts. Deserts are by no means uninteresting; still less are they useless. Deserts also serve to point the way whither we should be moving. Nowhere is all this more evident that in contemporary philosophy, in which the critical element has almost extinguished the speculative one, which, though by no means assuring the accomplishment of the creative act, is nevertheless its indispensable condition. Among the reasons for the kind of meaninglessness many of our contemporaries see in the term "God" is the fact that the conditions for the encouragement of human creativity are so enfeebled by various contemporary circumstances such as I have indicated that most people find it very difficult even to imagine what the nature of God could be. The notion that Nature might be the result of the voluntary self-diminishment of God, the renunciation of his power, is intelligible only to those who know the unspeakable anguish and exquisite joy that human creativity entails.

"The creation of heaven and earth," writes the Russian theologian Serge Bulgakov, ". . . is a voluntary self-diminution, a metaphysical 'kenosis', with respect to divinity itself: God places, side by side with his absolute being, the relative being with which he puts himself in relation, making himself its God and Creator." [2] Bulgakov wishes to stress that the world is not merely a divine accomplishment; "it is the revelation of the divine love that seeks to embrace also the nonexistent. . . . And it is not a gratuitous love . . . but a love making itself known in all its seriousness, its responsibility, its sacrifice, and also in its tragicalness: a love sacrificing, in its accomplishment, everything it possesses." [3]

These are provocative words. Can they lead us to a useful insight? We need not be put off by the Hegelian overtones of the language. We are asked to envisage a Triune God who, being identified with the Absolute, nevertheless by his creative act places himself in a state of relationship that entails his never-ending self-diminishment. Bulgakov, in conformity with traditional Eastern Orthodox emphasis, introduces the notion in a thoroughly trinitarian setting. The kenosis is no longer a special and anomalous soteriological wonder; it is involved in the creative act itself. God as Creator is kenotic Being.

Bulgakov was by no means alone in this interpretation of the creative act. Half a century ago a group of Anglican scholars were holding meetings to discuss theological questions. With one exception, they were all teaching theology at Oxford; the exception, F. H. Brabant, was teaching philosophy there before the influence of the Vienna Circle had begun to make itself felt. Their temper was orthodox and trinitarian. Brabant, in a contribution to the published result of these meetings, declared: "The only possible

[2] Serge Bulgakov, *Du Verbe incarné* (Paris: Aubier, 1943), p. 48. Translation mine.

[3] Ibid., p. 51.

formula which satisfies Christian needs by recognizing at
once God's supremacy and His real struggle in the world is
that of Self-limitation." [4] Going on to specify that he had in
mind no divine artist as in the *Timaeus* but a God who
creates "out of nothing," he pointed out that the *ex nihilo*
formula "can only mean 'nothing other than Himself.' " [5]
Disclaiming any ability to provide a metaphysical explana-
tion for so mysterious a notion, he nevertheless made an
observation that points as clearly as does Bulgakov in the
direction I propose to go. He wrote: "there is at least
nothing unthinkable in the view that Omnipotence should
be able to restrain itself as well as put itself forth. . . . The
idea expressed by the Self-limitation of God is that He puts
Himself, as it were, at a disadvantage. He lets Himself be
disappointed, insulted, rejected by His creatures." [6]

What all such writers saw in one way or another is that as
soon as we postulate a divine Being who creates the
universe we are forced to contend with the question why he
should do so. For since *ex hypothesi* he is in no way
dependent on that which he creates, we naturally ask why
he should create at all. Generally speaking, when we write
or cook or build, we do so because we have some need of
either the exercise or the result. Yet the more ability we
possess, the less need we have for any particular result or
exercise. I have sometimes advised young men and women
who have exhibited dangerous symptoms of writer's itch:
don't write if you can possibly help it. Some of the more
reflective perceive, however, that while they *could* abstain
they would not feel right in abstaining. Saint Martin of
Tours, who gave away half his cloak to a beggar, could have

[4] F. H. Brabant, "God and Time" in A. E. J. Rawlinson (ed.), *Essays on the
Trinity and the Incarnation* (London: Longmans, Green, 1928), p. 353. Cf. the
more recent work of Nelson Pike, *God and Timelessness* (New York: Schocken,
1970).

[5] Brabant, "God and Time," p. 353.

[6] Ibid., p. 353.

abstained. That is to say, we need not suppose he was so
enslaved to the compulsion to give away his clothing that he
could not have refrained from doing so even by a Herculean
effort of his will. No, the whole point of the story is that he
did not in the least relish the notion of parting with his
clothing, which he needed very much; but that nevertheless
he did part with it out of compassion for the beggar who
needed it more.

When I tell a young person not to write if he can help it,
of course I do not mean that an obsession to write is the
proper condition for writing. If he has an obsession to write
he should consult a psychiatrist. The proper condition for
writing, as for any creative act, is that you would much
prefer to play tennis or to watch television, yet you know
that you can and that you ought to write. In any truly
creative act I must not only agonize; I must give something
of myself away. Ability does not diminish the anguish of that
self-giving; on the contrary, the more ability I have, the
greater the travail needed for the creative act. If, then, I
could be "omnipotent" in the commonly understood sense
of "being able to do anything" (or at any rate anything not
contrary to my own nature), the anguish of my creative acts
would be infinitely increased. My need for any result or
exercise would be, however, infinitely diminished.

In Mahayana Buddhism, such notions are foreshadowed
in a different setting. The aim of the Buddhist life is to
eliminate all desire, which is the cause of *dukkha*, sorrow.
Some beings, however, who have achieved that detachment,
through the annihilation of all desire, and are ready,
therefore, to pass beyond into nirvanic bliss, tarry out of
love and compassion for suffering humanity. These bodhisattvas or little buddhas postpone their entrance into
nirvana to help those who call on them. Sometimes they
even descend in the guise of ministering angels and perform
deeds of compassion. In one way or another they elect to
function as saviors instead of enjoying the nirvanic bliss to

which they are already entitled. Here also, I think, in that relatively primitive climate of thought, one sees the nature of creativity, for the bodhisattvas are engaged in the creation of "new creatures"; that is, of the new beings they hope to create out of the desire-tormented beings in the world of *dukkha*. They are engaged in what, in Christian language, would be called redemptive process. They need not do what they do; yet they do it. Christ "came down from heaven"; yet he need not have done so. For God so to save creatures could be only an aspect or manifestation, however, of the tremendous act of creation "out of nothing other than himself."

The kenosis, traditionally understood as an interpretation of the incarnational mystery that appears at the heart of Christian dogma, may be considered in the larger context of divine creation. I propose, however, to go further still. I wish to consider kenosis as the root principle of Being. To call God kenotic Being is to specify what we mean by saying "God is love." I am proposing that by "God" we cannot mean Being that exercises omnipotence as an act of self-expansion, because (a) acts of self-expansion are in the long run self-destructive and in any case (b) if God is indeed omnipotent in the sense that he is subject to no limitation outside himself, he could not conceivably enhance his Being through self-expansion, for there would be nowhere into which an infinitely powerful Being could expand. Having nowhere to go by way of self-expansion he would still have infinitely available to him the way of self-limitation, self-abnegation.

What has been discussed in the preceding paragraph is by no means alien to our experience. We who have indeed plenty of room for self-expansion find that self-expansion by no means ever brings us in any way closer to God. When, however, we engage in self-limitation, self-denial, self-sacrifice, we do find that a new dimension of life opens up in such a way that we may choose to say it turns us God-ward.

In the very act of engagement in such self-abnegation we are actually finding out that if there be a God at all he must be much more characteristically engaged in kenotic acts than is commonly supposed.

The process of self-limitation that comes within the ambit of our own experience is adumbrated in the very act of man's first turning inwards from the external world. Primitive man, having been, like any other animal, habitually turned outwards to exercise his power, learns at last to turn inwards into the interior dimension of the life of the mind. Only then does he become truly human. Empirically, man does not look grander than the other animals. On the contrary, he cuts a poor figure by comparison with other mammals. He lacks the splendor of the lion and the magnificence of the tiger. He is incapable of the swift soaring elegance of the birds, the submarine capacity of the fish, and the resourceful agility of some of his own simian cousins. The size of his brain suggests superior cerebral power; but in itself it could not show man as radically better or "higher" than an elephant or a chimpanzee. Only through his invisible qualities, his unseen symbol-making and conceptualizing abilities, which give meaning to the noises he makes with his throat and mouth, is his superiority recognizable. It is within this dimension of his existence that he begins to discover that superior to the exercise of such physical powers as he possesses is his ability to renounce the use of power. Is not that why only humankind can laugh and weep?

So it is that man learns to turn away from uncontrolled aggression and piggish gluttony and savage lust toward the humane virtues and civilized restraints: toleration and sympathy, tenderness and compassion, discipline of the fiercer animal appetites. Gradually he asks not only the origin of the universe around him but the nature of the power that draws him into the newly discovered dimension within himself whose nature stands in such sharp contrast to that of the external world. More gradually still he learns the power of sacrificial love, apart from which all his attempts to conquer the world around him or to develop his human capacity are futile. If, at length, he sees that divine Being beckons him as the source of whatever it is that he is becoming, he is on his way to understanding that he is called upon to worship neither brute force nor sultanic dominion but the divine kenotic power of which his own experience of human sacrificial love provides, however feebly, the best analogue.

To say that God is sovereign is really a truism. The term "God" always means a Being who is in some way sovereign over all other beings. The question must be: if there be a God, *in what way* is he sovereign? Traditionally, Christianity provides the model of a God who is sovereign in the exercise of omnipotence but who nevertheless surprises us men and women by his uniquely astonishing act through which he "sends" his "only Son" to redeem us. The models traditionally provided suggest that that divine act is both unique and unexpected. That is why it was such a stumbling-block to the Jews and such foolishness to the Greeks. It is indeed a stumbling-block and foolishness to many; but, after all, there were some Jews who did not stumble over it and some Greeks who did not take it for folly. There have been some in every age, not only Christians but people of every religious heritage, who have seen, however dimly, that, whatever divine Being is, such must be his fundamental nature. That has not been, however, the commonly accepted understanding. A contemporary Japanese theologian does not exaggerate when he depicts the more common understanding as follows: ". . . God, against his nature, took an emergency measure and made Christ suffer for the redemption of sin." [7]

---

[7] K. Kitamori, *Theology of the Pain of God* (Richmond, Va.: John Knox Press, 1965), p. 45. A translation of the fifth edition of the Japanese original, *Kami no itami no shingaku* (Tokyo: Shinkyo Shuppansha, 1958).

The same author goes on to insist that, on the contrary, the Cross is not to be understood as external to God but as an act within God.[8]

So to state the case is to recognize that suffering is (to use classical Christian language) of the "essence" *(ousia)* of God. When the writer of the letter to the Hebrews tells us it was "fitting" to make Christ perfect through suffering,[9] he would seem to be telling us that the Cross is anything else other than a merciful deviation from the divine nature. On the contrary, the biblical view seems to be that it belongs to the heart of God, to the nature of the "Lamb" who keeps the roll of the living, written since the creation of the world *(apo kataboles kosmou)*.[10]

[8] Ibid.
[9] Heb. 2:10.
[10] Rev. 13:8.

CHAPTER VII

Freedom and
Necessity

*For the philosopher, then, the problem
of history and destiny is identical with
that of freedom and necessity. . . .
However philosophical reason may
define the concept of freedom, it always returns to the conclusion that
freedom, in so far as it is truly creative
and effective, must consist solely in the
recognition of a superior necessity and
in obedience to its laws. The only
question is in regard to the character of
this necessity.*

—Erich Frank, *Philosophical Understanding
and Religious Truth.*

OF all the theological puzzles that have troubled the
minds of thoughtful people, none has proved more notoriously intractable than that of divine predestination and
human freedom. The classic theologians have ingeniously
attempted to provide theological solutions purporting to
transcend the philosophical insolubility of the problem of
necessity and freedom. Nevertheless, wherever God is seen

as the omnipotent and immutable One, as He-who-ordains, all the basic philosophical difficulties to be found in the necessity-freedom problem rear their heads no less insistently in its theological counterpart.

The notion that I am in some sense free yet at the same time constrained by necessity (whether the necessity be of Nature or of God) is by any reckoning paradoxical. The man in the street, by a right instinct, perceives this. Moreover, the unconscious attachment of many contemporary philosophers as well as others to outmoded Newtonian, mechanistic models of the universe aggravates the confusion. Hume's difficulties about causation reflected his failure to recognize two distinct interpretative approaches: on the one hand, the forceful activities that bear down upon us; on the other, the *Gestalt*, the arrangement within which these forceful activities occur. In the activities themselves we see a power so strong, so blind, so unrelenting, that we call it necessity, since it comes to us so inexorably as to make plain our lack of choice. When my hands are securely locked in steel manacles and my feet in fetters, the question of my walking or not walking simply does not arise: I am of necessity immobilized. Born on a certain day, in a certain place, and of certain parents, the question whether I might have preferred another date or place or parentage is likewise only a pseudo-question, for by no means could I ever change them. Only from the *Gestalt* can any causal laws be derived; yet the *Gestalt* does not *do* anything. It is we who "do things": but in doing them are we mere puppets, as the determinists would have us, or do we rightfully claim some degree of freedom of choice as agents?

The thoroughgoing determinist refuses to allow any genuine freedom of choice at all. On his view I am indeed a puppet. My motives cannot properly be called good or bad, for they simply reflect my psychological state of affairs, which in turn reflects the sociological state of affairs in the society in which I have been reared, and that society is likewise a product of the biological condition of the human race, which is likewise the outcome of other natural forces, and so forth. Such a determinist invests Nature with power to determine everything that ever can happen. Plainly, on any view of this kind, there is no room for any kind of freedom at all. Nature not only governs everything by her inexorable law; she applies that law with all the ruthlessness of a despot. Psychologically, sociologically, economically, and physically, I simply *behave.* The nature of my behavior is a proper subject for certain specialists to analyze and describe; but no judgment is possible on whether I have behaved well or ill, except in the sense in which a combustion engine behaves well or ill; that is, whether it serves the purpose of a driver who uses it or fails to serve that purpose. Though there is no freedom in a universe where everything is so thoroughly determined, there is still a wide spectrum of forms of slavery; but if ropes and chains are equally constricting, whether I am held down by one or the other can be of no importance to me.

People commonly suspect that a universe governed by a predestinating deity is in the same case. Despite the protestations of many theologians to the contrary, we may well ask whether popular suspicions be not well founded. Does it make any difference to the determinative force that grips everything, whether it be called Nature or God? If I am totally bereft of all freedom of choice, can it matter to me by what or by whom I am constrained? Do I care who is my jailor? Do I rejoice that it is not Smith but Jones, or wish it might be Brown rather than White? Surely not. It could make no difference, since the result would be the same. What makes the theologian claim otherwise is the belief behind his contention that while Nature in her omnipotence is blind, God in his omnipotence is omniscient and omnibenevolent. Now, it may be psychologically solacing to me to feel that the despot whose puppet I am is noble and intelligent rather than mindless and dull; but the solace, if any, is not a solace that is likely to endure very long. If you and I should each be pinned against the wall by a car, you would be little comforted by the thought that while I was being crushed by a plebeian Ford you were being mangled by a patrician Rolls Royce. You would know that you were going to end up as dead as I. If, then, I am to be an abject slave, I cannot much care whether my master is to be called Nature or God.

In fact, however, when the theologian protests that predestination is (appearances notwithstanding) neither a metaphysical nor a moral determinism but something far more mysterious, his denial always issues from his belief that, in the case of God, a mitigating factor so modifies the despotism of God as to allow an element of human freedom. How the two are to be reconciled is admitted to be difficult; but at any rate predestination, whatever it be, and however it be related to human freedom, is to be seen as different from naturalistic determinism. It is the character of God that makes the difference.

Skeptics, when they are patient enough to listen with attention if not sympathy to such theological contentions, characteristically say in effect: "All right, then, let us grant for argument's sake that the character of the divine Being introduces a difference, and let us suppose, further, that the difference it introduces is specific enough to enable us to estimate at least very roughly what degree of human freedom might be allowed. What will the predestination-freedom traffic bear? Could it be, say, 80% divine predestination and foreknowledge and 20% human freedom? Surely not. With such a model, unless both the predestination and the freedom are somehow complete, both terms lose whatever meaning might have been imputed to them. The same kind of difficulty arises with the notion of divine omnipotence. God, being omnibenevolent, is able to do anything, yet he permits evil to emerge. Why does not he construct a universe in which hideous accidents such as an earthquake in the middle of San Francisco or Mexico City simply would not occur and in which the parents of those whom God, through his foreknowledge, sees destined to turn into malicious rotters, simply would not beget or conceive them?"

If predestination means predetermination (and theologians have never been very convincing when they have denied that it does), then God must be said to be the cause of whatever occurs. That conforms, of course, to the traditionally familiar cosmology of Aristotle: God is the First Cause. Saint Thomas, bound to this metaphysical view at least as much for an Aristotelian reason as for any biblical one, faced the difficulties with it that have always confronted theists. God does not will evil; yet it enters in. God hates sin; yet he allows people to do it. The reason adduced for the divine permissiveness is the attractive yet by no means universally persuasive one classically provided by Augustine: God wants his creatures to love him freely, so they must be free not to love him; otherwise they would be automata and incapable of the only kind of love acceptable to God. But what kind of freedom could it be that can enter into a universe predetermined by God or Nature? How could I ever be free enough for my love to qualify as acceptable to God? Theologians who have adequately faced such difficulties have always ended by having to mitigate divine causation, and even then the rest of their account represents a human freedom so attenuated that it seems only to augment the confusion. One cannot easily avoid the conclusion that the freedom claimed is a metaphysical fiction awaiting Occam's knife. Divine causation and human freedom do not sit well together at any point.

There is an obvious alternative; but it is not one that theists have generally entertained. In so far as the universe might be said to have a "law" at all, it would be a law not administered in terms of causation but a law administered in terms of freedom. That would be to say that freedom is a principle of Being itself. It could only mean that creaturely freedom would always be commensurate with the achievement of a capacity for freedom. By way of analogy we might take the traditional notion of extension in space. If, conceptualizing in an old-fashioned way, we were to think of extension in space as a "law" for every physical body, we should have to recognize that the law could apply only in the measure that such a body is capable of occupying space; an elephant has a larger capacity than a fly; yet even a sub-microscopic virus occupies some space, and in doing so it may make its presence far more mischievously effective on me than any elephant so far has been able to make his. Similarly, we may say that if freedom is a law or principle of Being itself, it can apply to creaturely beings such as ourselves only in so far as we have achieved the capacity to exercise that freedom.

That such capacity for freedom is a reality that human beings can conspicuously manifest, though comparatively few individuals have so far actually achieved the conditions necessary for its full manifestation is, of course, the insight associated with existentialism, whether that of religious men such as Kierkegaard and Marcel or of nihilists like Nietzsche and Sartre. Pascal, that most penetrating expositor of the same theme two centuries before even Kierkegaard was writing on it, saw the tragi-comic absurdity of man, whose one foot is caught fast in the mud while the other leaps out high among the stars. "What monster, then, is man?" [1] He is monstrous because he is a creature in the travail of discovering his capacity for freedom.

It is easy to contrast the determinists and the existentialists, seeing the former as the champions of necessity and the

---

[1] Pascal, *Pensées*, 434: "Quelle chimère est-ce donc l'homme? Quelle nouveauté, quel monstre, quel chaos, quel sujet de contradiction, quel prodige! Juge de toutes choses, imbécile ver de terre; dépositaire du vrai, cloaque d'incertitude et d'erreur; gloire et rebut de l'univers."

latter as contenders for freedom of choice. In fact, however, both recognize the paradox in which freedom and necessity seem to demand recognition yet seem also irreconcilable. The existentialists, not least Sartre, are as deeply impressed by the power of circumstance as ever were Marx and Freud. Contrariwise, Marx, while recognizing that Nature "always remains a realm of necessity," goes on to say: "Beyond it begins that development of human power which is its own end, the true realm of freedom which, however, can flourish only upon that realm of necessity as its basis." [2] That sounds, indeed, more like a libertarian than a determinist manifesto! We even hear Marxist talk of "humanity's leap from the realm of necessity into the realm of freedom." [3] The difference between the existentialists and the determinists would seem to lie in their emphases and their interpretation of the nature of the struggle between necessity and freedom, rather than in any radical difference in the way they see the fundamental nature of Being.

Theologians have too generally acquiesced in the naturalist presuppositions common to an Engels and a Sartre, and have only exchanged "God" for "Nature" as the name of necessity's agent. So, to patient piety, earthquakes and cancers become "God's will." Even sin becomes felicitous (*felix culpa*), since without it redemption could not have occurred. Then the mystery is: how can there be any human freedom at all? Or else, if there be any freedom, is it not the merest tokenism? Luther and Calvin seem, at least sometimes, to represent such an attitude of what might even be

[2] Karl Marx, *Capital*, Vol. III (Chicago: Charles H. Kerr and Company, 1909), pp. 954f. Marx characteristically says, of course, that "freedom in this field cannot consist of anything else but the fact that socialized man, the associated producers, regulate their interchange with nature rationally. . . ." This does not affect, however, the point I am making here. For a full treatment of the problem of freedom in Marxism, with bibliography, see James J. O'Rourke, *The Problem of Freedom in Marxist Thought* (Holland: D. Reidel, 1974).

[3] Friedrich Engels, *Handbook of Marxism* (London: Victor Gollancz, 1936), p. 299.

called Christian determinism, while the more fashionable tendency among lively Christian thinkers in our own time is toward what is often called Christian existentialism, with its stress on freedom. One may well question, however, whether the Freuds and the Marxes have gone far enough with their determinism, and one certainly ought to ask whether the Christians may not have been too timid in pressing Kierkegaard's existentialist theme.

What does "necessity" mean on such a view, whether it be thought to spring from Nature or from God? It means plainly that such is the source of all things, call it what you will, that whatever occurs could not not-occur and indeed could not occur in any way other than the way in which it does occur. On such a view that which is true of the history of rocks and the evolution of reptiles is equally true of the history of man. We may wax as poetic as we please about "freedom"; but it remains no less a fantasy, no less an illusion, than Freud has repeatedly called it.[4] Where the religious man thinks of God simply as "he who ordaineth," that is, "he who despotically commands," freedom (for all that he may call it a mystery) becomes no less an illusion. The might of God overwhelms, whether in withholding or bestowing. Well might Job remind his friends that if God "tears down, none can rebuild; if he shuts a man in, none can open. If he withholds the waters, they dry up; if he sends them out, they overwhelm the land."[5] For all man's pretensions his lot is worse than that of a vegetable or a plant: "For there is hope for a tree, if it be cut down, that it will sprout again, and that its shoots will not cease. . . . But man dies, and is laid low; man breathes his last, and where is he? As waters fall from a lake, and a river wastes away and dries up, so man lies down and rises not again. . . ."[6]

---

[4] E.g., Sigmund Freud, *Collected Papers*, Vol. IV (London: 1925), p. 388.
[5] Job 12:14–15 (RSV).
[6] Job 14:7, 10–12 (RSV).

When God is seen as "the Omnipotent King who ordaineth," our proper attitude toward him is closely akin to the naturalist's attitude toward Nature. Grace is as irresistible as is sunshine in a tropical desert or darkness in an Alaskan winter. Not only have bullets soldiers' names on them; the script for every act I perform has been written long ago in heaven. That I like to think otherwise is but part of my plight, part of my inheritance of original sin. Not only am I, according to Sartre's taunt, *jeté là, comme ça;* not only am I thrown[7] into the world without my asking; I am mocked by a thirst for knowledge, whether of Nature or of God, that in the end leads me only to the admission that I have no more say in the unfolding of my life than I have in the circumstances of my birth or the certainty of my death. In short, the poignancy of my human condition lies in the fact that the more I know of the universe and of myself and the better I understand how I stand in relation to what I take to be the fundamental ground, the core of all things, the more I see the futility of my pretensions to free choice. Like the goose in Kierkegaard's parable, who grew sick and died of introspection, I might have been better just to have remained as untroubled as the other geese who grew fat and were duly eaten on Martinmas Eve.

That would be true if the freedom I claim were in the last resort a grand illusion. If God exerts his power in the manner of a despotic sultan, my hope of escape from it is as foolish as my dream of suspending the "laws of Nature." "Can you find out the limit of the Almighty? It is higher than heaven—what can you do? Deeper than Sheol—what can you know?" [8] The more you know, the more you know you are powerless. As the ancient proverb has it: man proposes, God disposes. If, however, my freedom of choice could be a reality that in the last resort might stand unchallenged by Nature or by God, the whole situation

---

[7] Heidegger's word is *geworfen.*
[8] Job 11:7–8 (RSV).

would be completely changed. That, I believe, is impossible unless God can be understood to exercise his power very differently from the way in which his almightiness has been traditionally presented. There is no doubt that the groundwork for what is needed is provided in the biblical documents of the Christian faith, which, if they attest anything at all, attest that God is love. The implicates of that affirmation, however, have not been fully drawn. On the contrary, the affirmation has been smothered under a vast weight of outmoded metaphysical presupposition. The recognition of what the affirmation implies is of crucial importance for the resolution of the traditional paradox of necessity and freedom. Augustine caught a glimpse of the solution; but he did not carry it far enough. To provide room for human freedom of choice, or indeed for any kind of freedom within a theistic system, God must not only occasionally restrain himself in the exercise of his power; he must never exercise it at all except in support of love, and love without freedom is impossible. Love *is* the abdication of power. God is not only He-who-is; God is He-who-abdicates. Deeply provocative are the words of Simone Weil: "Love consents to all and commands only those who consent. Love is abdication. God is abdication." [9] When she also asserts that what the natural scientists are studying is the impersonal providence of God,[10] she provides a further clue for the resolution of the paradox. We shall do well to look closely at the implications of these characteristically cryptic epigrams of that twentieth-century genius in the light of what she has to say about necessity.

Her understanding of the nature of necessity constitutes one of the most illuminating aspects of the astonishingly

[9] Simone Weil, *La Connaissance surnaturelle* (Paris: Gallimard, 1950), p. 267: "L'Amour consent à tout et ne commande qu'à ceux qui y consente. L'Amour est abdication. Dieu est abdication."

[10] Ibid., p. 319.

vast spectrum of her thought. God is Being, and the only necessity in him is the necessity that is identical with his goodness. In abdicating in order to create us, he permits that necessity to yield in favor of another, "blind" necessity to take over and reign in his stead. That necessity is indifferent to good. If we ask why God so acts as to grant this power of attorney, as we might call it, to that "blind" necessity of the "natural" world, the answer must be that doing so is an implicate of creation itself, for without that grant to "blind" necessity the creature could not exercise his freedom and so find his way to God. The creature would be in a position analogous to that of an infant who, being exposed to only one kind of sensation, say, warmth of a certain degree, could not identify or reflect upon that sensation. The creature would lack anything with which to compare it.[11] As Kant showed, relations are necessary for any kind of knowledge. So without a world of "blind" necessity we could not know "how to be free," and that is the only way divine love can create. Here is her way of putting her exhilarating stance:

> Relentless necessity, wretchedness, distress, the crushing burden of poverty and of labour which wears us out, cruelty, torture, violent death, constraint, disease—all these constitute divine love. It is God who in love withdraws from us so that we can love him. For if we were exposed to the direct radiance of his love, without the protection of space, of time, and of matter, we should be evaporated like water in the sun; there would not be enough "I" in us to make it possible to surrender the "I" for love's sake. Necessity is the screen set between God and us so that we can be. It is for us to pierce through the screen so that we cease to be.[12]

[11] See my *The Sense of Absence* (Philadelphia: J. B. Lippincott, 1968), for a discussion of the theme that God is better known through his absence than through his presence.

[12] Simone Weil, *Gravity and Grace* (London: Routledge and Kegan Paul, 1947), p. 28.

Such a view affects our whole philosophy of history and our understanding of time:

> God himself cannot prevent what has happened from having happened. What better proof that the creation is an abdication? What greater abdication of God than is represented by time? We are abandoned in time. God is not in time. Creation and original sin are only two aspects, which are different for us, of a single act of abdication by God. And the Incarnation, the Passion, are also aspects of this act. God emptied himself of his divinity and filled us with a false divinity. Let us empty ourselves of it. This act is the purpose of the act by which we were created. At this very moment God, by his creative will, is maintaining me in my existence, in order that I may renounce it.[13]

To say that He-who-is is not He-who-ordains but He-who-abdicates is to say about the nature of Being something that Christians do not commonly expect to hear. It may even sound radically different from what Christian theologians, as heirs of a special development of Greek thought, have usually felt compelled to have their audiences assume.

Theologians have generally acquiesced in, if not stressed, the notion that the first thing to recognize in God the Creator is that, as the source of all that is, he exists of necessity. He is, in Plato's phrase, *to ontōs on*. He is *ens realissimum*. From a Christian standpoint, however, saying all that would seem to be no less of a truism than is, from the standpoint of a nihilist, the notion that existence is a fact. The nihilist treats as a pseudo-question (or non-question) the question mentioned earlier, which was posed by Leibniz and more recently by Heidegger as the most profound philosophical question that can be asked: "Why is there anything at all and not just nothing?" [14] The nihilist is

---

[13] Simone Weil, *First and Last Notebooks*, trans. R. Rees (London: Oxford University Press, 1970), p. 140. Cf. her *Gravity and Grace*, p. 30.

[14] Leibniz, *Opera Philosophica* (ed. J. E. Erdmann, 1840, Faksimile Druck,

right from his viewpoint, according to which existence is simply that which is given. It has no nature or character *per se*, and so in it there is nothing for a nihilist to discuss. One may usefully discuss the phenomena of existence and even try to interpret them; but one can no more discuss existence itself than one can discuss nothing. The fact that without it there would be nothing to discuss at all, and nobody to discuss anything, does not affect the situation as the nihilist sees it. At best he sees no need to do more about that fact than perfunctorily note it and go on to what can be usefully noticed in and argued about the phenomena.

The notion that God necessarily exists may be treated by a Christian theologian very much as existence is treated by nihilists and positivists. The question then arises: what is the nature of the Being who exists of necessity? In contrast to the characterless existence in the nihilist's model, the Being acclaimed by Christians not only has a character but communicates this character in all his acts and to all his creation. Traditionally, theologians, borrowing ancient metaphysical notions, have tended to begin all accounts of his attributes by assigning to the Being who is at the heart of all things the character of being the primary cause of everything that is non-God, describing him sometimes as the ever-outpouring fountain, sometimes as the ground on which all else stands. Then they go on to recount the biblical testimony that he is almighty, omniscient, omnibenevolent, and so forth, and that the Bible and the Fathers, in poetic outbursts, occasionally even say roundly that God is love. Theologians ought rather to notice the necessity of God (as nihilists might notice the fact of existence) and then immediately go on to specify what is his essential nature. The biblical and patristic testimony is plain: God is indeed incomprehensible, "past finding out";

Renate Vollbrecht, Anton Hain, 1959), p. 148. Heidegger poses a similar question in *Existence and Being* (Chicago: Henry Regnery Co., 1949), p. 380.

nevertheless, if anything at all is revealed about him in human terms it is contained in affirmations such as "God is love." If we started out in this fashion, everything we went on to say about almightiness and omniscience and the like would be subordinate to the primary affirmation. Whatever the power that is in God, it could not be sultanic. It could not be power such that the power of a Napoleon or an Alexander the Great could be even a farfetched analogue of it. Similarly, if one began with the primary affirmation "God is love," one could not easily go on to the customary exacerbation of the confusion by allowing anyone to suppose that predicating omniscience of God is in any way like calling him a vast cosmic computer or a gargantuan encyclopaedia-cum-directory of the universe. We must examine more closely, however, what it means to say that God is best symbolized as sacrificial love.

It means above all that we must repudiate every symbol of God that represents him as the first cause. For if God is properly symbolized as sacrificial love (that is to say, if sacrificial love is the fundamental principle of Being), then God must be represented in such a way that he never at any point interferes with his creatures. Even *en archē*, in giving them the condition of their existence, in bestowing on them their participatory status of Being, he puts no restraint on them. He lets them be. The earthworm is left to become what it will. True, it would be a foolish worm were it to try to do it all at once or even in a thousand years, for the conditions in which we are all placed, worms and humans alike, are not conquered without yielding to them, as all wise men have learned.

To say that God, in the act of creation, imposes necessity on all his creatures is simply to specify what freedom is and what are its entailments. Necessity and freedom are correlative terms. Such is freedom that it is meaningless apart from the necessity within which it is exercised. We can neither choose any course of conduct nor do any action except within a framework that presents us with obstacles. What the obstacles are can be of little if any importance, however much we may be tempted to think otherwise when they are confronting us. Asking whether one set of circumstances or kind of obstacle is "better" for "producing" freedom is like arguing the merits of Latin over Sanskrit or German as a good discipline for developing a student's critical faculties or a discriminating linguistic taste. If I know a great deal about physics but very little about chemistry, chemistry will be a more difficult subject for me; but it will be also what I need far more to learn. Necessity is what is needed for an agent to attain freedom. To attain freedom is to acquire power; but only when freedom is cheaply bought and so, we might even say, of a low quality, will the agent wantonly exercise the power. Indeed, whenever we see the self-limitation of power we know the self-limiting agent has bought it dearly. None more than the manumitted slave prizes his liberty.

Necessity, then, far from being a hindrance, is the indispensable condition for the development of freedom. As we shall consider in the next chapter, it often assumes fearsome forms; but the terror these induce diminishes as we realize, in combat with the terrifying obstacles, the quality of the freedom that our victory over them makes available to us. God in no way hinders his creatures in their struggle for development. Not only does the sun shine upon the just and the unjust; God lets the rebellious shake their fists at him, and even deny his existence, as freely as the devout adore and praise him. He never exerts any kind of pressure on his creatures.

What then are the obstacles that do hinder us? The pressures we feel are the pressures arising partly from our own and partly from other creatures' insufficiently self-abnegating character. Wherever I exert power I find myself constrained by the pressure of all that is around me exercising power after its own fashion. Only in so far as I learn to abdicate do I cease to feel that pressure, for then I have transcended it and so escaped from it by realizing in myself the fundamental principle of Being.

So all that exists is free in the sense that it is unconstrained by any external force that is "out to destroy" it. Even the rivers and the rocks have the universal capacity for freedom that belongs to all creatures. A powerful instinct, however, the instinct of self-preservation, leads all beings to assert themselves, to fight and even to destroy, for that is our own way of trying to learn the secret of Being. The learning process is long and painful. We might illustrate it by an analogy. Suppose ten thousand people who had always been accustomed to living in very spacious surroundings, each with a vast estate at his disposal, were to be suddenly arrested and squeezed together in a single ship. Their first instinct would be to assert themselves and extend or spread themselves as much as possible, trying to make themselves as large as they could and so displace other competitors. In so doing they would find, of course, that they invited the hostility of the others who would be similarly engaged in vying for survival. Only as they learned that the "clever thing to do" is in fact the opposite, that is, to try to make themselves smaller, to empty themselves, would they make possible their individual survival and so discover the secret of their salvation.

A corollary of this parable is that God is better symbolized by the microcosm than by the macrocosm. The symbol for God that Pascal once proposed, a point moving at infinite speed, much better exhibits God's abdicating nature than do either the traditional "throne-in-the-sky" or the more fashionable "ground-to-stand-on" symbols. Contrary to those who applaud the Eastern Churches for their exaltation of Easter and their minimizing of Good Friday, and who correspondingly deprecate the Latin emphasis on the Cross, Calvary is a good symbol of God. At any rate, our own freedom is to be won, not by imitations of sultanic omnipotence but, rather, by self-restraint, even self-empty-ing. No cross, no crown: Kenosis is the only way to freedom, for it is the principle of Being itself, the principle of Him-who-abdicates. The whole universe may be seen, then, as groaning and travailing, to use Paul's words, because creatures are stifling themselves by their own contradiction of the basic principle of Being.

That is by no means to deny the appositeness of the He-who-is formula. On the contrary it is to specify the character of the is-ness. Nor is the old fountain-symbol a wrong one, for the is-ness is indeed an outpouring. Never-theless, it is not a wanton outpouring but the sacrificial outpouring of kenotic love and its power is kenotic power. God may then be seen to be thoroughly permissive. Yet, as we shall see, his permissiveness is matched by his readiness to intervene when our supplications are made by those who are in the kenotic way. As the Hebrew psalmist sang in what we now call the *Miserere*:

> *My sacrifice is this broken spirit,*
> *You will not scorn this crushed and broken heart.*[15]

Were the divine power as it has been more typically understood, I might then be in the traditional quandary: "I am expected to exercise my God-given freedom and assume the responsibility that is its correlative; yet who am I to suppose I can change what God ordains?" I would maintain, on the contrary, that both the Augustinians and the Pelagians have been right; only the presuppositions they had inherited and that they passed on were inadequate. God's grace does overwhelm and overtake; but the overtak-ing is part of my running away from God. It is I who, in fleeing from God, discover the kenotic nature of divine Being. It is I who, in seeking out God by "good works"

---

[15] Ps. 51:17 (JB).

discover in another way that same self-emptying secret. What I am discovering, whether through Augustinian means or Pelagian method, is that the omnipotence of God is the power of love, the *amor qui omnia vincit,* and that though God does not arbitrarily interfere in the struggles of his creatures, he is always omnisciently at the ready, when we are, to assist us in the discovery of the almightiness of kenotic power. To say that God is omnipotent can only mean that nothing diminishes his love.[16]

The "ground of being" and *actus purus* symbols remain, nevertheless, useful. For Being, in order to be self-emptying, must have a self to empty, as the ocean, in order to ebb and flow, must also be an ocean. The procedural error that has proved so misleading in theology arises when, instead of beginning with the datum that an ocean is of such a nature that it ebbs and flows, and Being is of such a nature that it is kenotic, we mistakenly talk as though an ocean is expected to do otherwise but, wonderful to relate, it ebbs and flows. That God is kenotic cannot be the solution to a particular problem that emerges in the midst of a sea of perplexities about the ways of God to man. It can be nothing if not a way of expressing the nature of Being itself. Once that ontic fact is grasped, necessity becomes a truism, and freedom that which we achieve through the exercise of kenotic power which, for every door that is closed to us, opens a thousand others.

[16] See W. D. Hudson, *Philosophy,* Vol. 39, No. 147 (January 1964), pp. 24–25.

CHAPTER VIII

Solution to the Problem of Evil

As sure as God ever puts his children in the furnace, he will be in the furnace with them.

—C. H. Spurgeon, *Privileges of Trial.*

FOR those who subscribe to any form of theistic belief, there can be no more intransigent difficulty than the problem of evil. Christians are not alone, of course, in having to face it. It arises wherever God is acclaimed as almighty while at the same time he is said to be all-loving. Such is also characteristic Jewish teaching, vividly expressed, for instance, in the following lines which, in their Aramaic form, are still chanted in Jewish synagogues on the first day of Shevuoth, before the reading of the Torah:

> *Could we with ink the ocean fill,*
> > *And were the heavens of parchment made,*
> *Were every stalk on earth a quill*
> > *And every man a scribe by trade,*
> *To write the love of God above*
> > *Would drain the ocean dry,*

Nor could the scroll contain the whole,
Though stretch'd from sky to sky.[1]

The *unde malum* question (whence comes evil?), which Boethius, in prison, put to the Lady Philosophy, had been asked even more poignantly many centuries earlier by Job. Various interpretations of theism, reminiscent of the "divine artist" theory in the *Timaeus*, which have gained favor in some quarters in modern times, have attempted to mitigate the thrust of the difficulty by suggesting that God faces conditions not of his own making, so that his power is limited by something external to himself. On this view, responsibility for the presence of evil in the universe cannot be imputed to God, since, all-loving though he be, he has to wrestle with a recalcitrant stuff, out of which is made all that is non-God, and in that stuff the origin of the canker is to be found. This view is, however, despite the protestations of its champions, a dualism rather than a theism. Biblical testimony tries to overcome the problem in its own way through the notion of Lucifer or Satan; but that only throws the problem back once again to God: Why did not God arrange things so that angels could not fall and turn into devils? Had he but chosen to do so, Satan could not have emerged.

Professor Mackie has put the objection in modern terms in a simple, not to say simplistic, way:

> If there is no logical impossibility in a man's freely choosing the good on one, or on several occasions, there cannot be a logical impossibility in his freely choosing the good on every occasion. God was not, then, faced with the choice of making innocent automata and making beings who, in acting freely, would sometimes go wrong: there was open to him the obviously

---

[1] The lines are from the Akdamuth. Shevuoth, which commemorates the giving of the Law to Moses, comes seven weeks after the Passover. The Christian Pentecost, ensuing similarly after Easter, is its counterpart.

better possibility of making beings who would act freely but always go right.[2]

Professor Antony Flew has argued along similar lines.[3] The believer's faith is that all will come right in the Kingdom of God; but as Mackie asks, why such a long way round?[4]

To anyone who has understood at all the testimony of the Bible and the Fathers it must be plain that Mackie and Flew are using an artificial model that is radically alien to anything that could be in the mind of anyone who takes seriously the affirmation that God is love. Unfortunately, traditional theology, while recognizing that believers do have an answer in their hearts, has not provided one in an intellectual form that would be generally intelligible to their minds. On the contrary, the traditional formulations seem only to compound the difficulties.

Innumerable attempts have been made to try to solve the puzzle: How can a God of love who is all-powerful permit conditions in which evil and sin are ever able to emerge at all? In respect of sin, Saint Augustine provided an answer that was indeed very perspicacious in its way. He argued that, because God wants his creatures to love him freely, he must allow them freedom of choice: to love him or to hate him. Love that is forced is not the kind of love he wants, and for the kind he wants the creature must be free to choose whether he will give that love or withhold it. Nevertheless, with a model that so exalts the notion of divine omnipotence, he invites the question: God can do anything not contrary to his nature, and his nature is one of omnibenevolence, so why can't he create beings who will in fact exercise their will affirmatively, loving him as he

[2] J. L. Mackie, "Evil and Omnipotence," *Mind*, LXIV (April 1955), p. 209.

[3] A. Flew, "Divine Omnipotence and Human Freedom," in *New Essays in Philosophical Theology*, ed. A. Flew and A. MacIntyre (New York: Macmillan Co., 1955).

[4] J. L. Mackie, "Theism and Utopia," *Philosophy* XXXVII (April 1962), p. 154.

deserves all the time? One can easily enough imagine an animal so healthy that, without injury to its freedom, it would be impervious to disease and would therefore always act in a healthy way. *Ex hypothesi* only a morally sick mind could hate God, so why could not God create minds and wills which, being healthy, would always act healthily? That is, in essence, the Mackie-Flew type of objection, so far as moral evil is concerned.

In respect of what some have called "surd" evil, that is, evil that seems to point to a fundamentally irrational element in the universe itself, the difficulties are, if anything, even greater. Some interesting theodicies have been proposed, among which that of Leibniz is probably at once the most celebrated and the most notoriously criticized. Such theodicies presuppose the model we have inherited from the formulations of a Hellenistic mould of thought. They all face the difficulty that, once God is said to be all-powerful, no amount of exegesis will help, so long as "power" is understood in the terms to which we are accustomed when we think of human power. An all-powerful deity could have ordered things so as to prevent the emergence of evil, natural or moral. Why did not God exercize his power at that most crucial point?

Saint Thomas provided an impressive answer for the thirteenth century: God cannot do anything contrary to his own nature. Today we need a more radical answer, and at this stage no such answer can possibly be obtained without a radical re-examination of the basic models with which we have been working. In particular we must re-examine what can be meant by an infinite degree of power, as power is commonly understood. The notion of an infinite degree of power, as we understand it in ordinary human terms (the power *to do* things), is, if intelligible at all, monstrous. Power is by its very nature limited. As soon as we try to conceive of an unlimited degree of it and then ascribe such unlimited power to God, we make him seem a monster. That such a monster should then be also omnibenevolent seems so unlikely as to demand the suspension of the intellect that proposes to accept the doctrine. The total picture is not coherent. True, we ought not to expect to understand God; but at least what is said about him should not be inconceivable or monstrous even to sympathetic hearers. Still, Thomas was groping in the right direction: God cannot do anything contrary to his nature of letting-be.

Besides the ambiguity in the term "power" there is also, as everyone acquainted with the history of ideas knows, another ambiguity in the term "goodness." In a theistic system, the goodness of God is intrinsic and inalienable, and the goodness of creatures is often presented as though it were received intact from God, though subject to loss or diminishment through sin. On the contrary, this view arises from a confusion that compounds the misunderstanding about divine power. God, in bringing a creature into being, bestows, of course, the graciousness that inheres in Being. As the nature of Being is dynamic, however, the creature must acquire for himself that goodness the attainment of which his freedom makes possible. Attempts to solve the problem of evil have been vitiated by failure to grasp the implications of the character of Being, which is dynamic in goodness, love, and power. Neither heroes nor saints come ready-made. True, the great Augustinian insistence on divine prevenience and our creaturely dependence on the divine initiative is not to be underestimated. It is one of the greatest insights in the history of Christian thought. There is enough to do it justice, however, in the recognition of the divine act of bringing his creatures into existence at all. There is also much that serves that purpose, as we shall consider later, in the Christian doctrine of Providence.

The history of the problem of evil has been ably presented in recent times by John Hick, with some proposals for its solution.[5] The late Austin Farrer devoted some of his extraordinarily versatile genius to a consideration of the problem, to which he brought not only an exceptionally incisive mind but also the profound understanding of a deeply touched life and heart.[6] Yet though these and other great minds have come very close to the nub of the problem, few have penetrated deeply enough to touch its core.

Among those who have done so, one of the most remarkable is Simone Weil. Like Bonhoeffer, she was cut off too early to allow the development of her thought: she was only thirty-four when, in 1943, she died.[7] Nevertheless, her writings forcefully direct our attention to a point repeatedly made: wherever religion represents God as exercising power universally, it may be taken to be false religion. This view may appear under the guise of Christianity or some other monotheistic religion; it is none the less false. Indeed, at this vital point even a non-monotheistic religion is to be preferred, as closer to true Christian doctrine, if only it does not fall into that error. For religions that do so err are idolatrous. They make an idol out of the exercise of what I have been calling sultanic power. Only those religions are true, she says, that have a concept of the divine renunciation. God is indeed, according to her, the cause of all that exists; but "he consents not to command it, though he has the power to do so. Instead he leaves two other forces to rule in his place. On the one hand there is the blind necessity attaching to matter, including the psychic matter of the soul, and on the other the autonomy essential to thinking persons." [8]

[5] John Hick, *Evil and the God of Love* (New York: Harper and Row, 1966).

[6] Austin Farrer, *Love Almighty and Ills Unlimited* (New York: Doubleday and Company, 1961).

[7] In her earlier work she exhibits considerable interest in social questions. In her last year the mystical element that pervades all her work seems to absorb her completely.

[8] Simone Weil, *Waiting on God*, trans. E. Craufurd (London: Collins, Fontana Books, 1959), p. 114.

These are suggestive words. Why the "blind necessity"? Why the "autonomy essential to thinking persons"? The necessity cannot but be a necessity within the structure of Being itself. If God is love, his Being cannot be monolithic or static; Being itself must be structured and dynamic. That is the truth that one aspect of the doctrine of the Trinity as traditionally formulated sought to recognize. Indeed, the doctrine of the Trinity might be accounted a protest against the view that the Being of God is unstructured. So deeply entrenched in ancient thought is this latter view that not only is it later adopted uncritically into Islamic thought; both Maimonides and Saint Thomas, when they were seeking to be "philosophical" rather than "theological," stress so much the unity and simplicity of divine Being as to make the doctrine of the Trinity seem the declaration of Christian faith rather than a philosophical statement about the Being of God. Thomas is saying, in effect: "Reason shows that the Being of God must be simple and therefore unstructured, as both the pagans and the Arabs saw in their own way, and as Maimonides reminded us; nevertheless, through revelation, Christian faith acknowledges that God, without injury to Reason, has found a way of transcending what Reason would expect." Thomas thought like that because he shared the presupposition of all thoughtful people of his day that the structured must be supported by the unstructured, that is, by the simplicity of the Being of God.

We need not so conceptualize. To talk of Being as structured and dynamic does not mean that it lacks stability. On the contrary, it is a way of saying that the divine love *is* the stability at the core of all things. There is nowhere else to look for it. How could there be, if God is love? That we should ever have supposed otherwise is due to a deeply ingrained presupposition that anything supportive of the universe must be something static. If God is love, he cannot stand aloof to be the ground of all things; he can be the ground of all things only in his self-giving love. We could not surely be traducing biblical testimony or Christian faith were we to go so far as to say that God cannot even know how *not* to love. The false model we tend to have is of One who stands secure, alone, and aloof, who nevertheless, having an omnibenevolent nature, goes forth to create, yet whose Being is never radically affected. Since, however, such a God would engage neither in sacrifice nor in risk, he could not be the God of love that the New Testament proclaims, for without risk or sacrifice nothing is worthy to be called love. Such is the paradox of Being that nowhere does God manifest his power more clearly than when he appears in weakness and humility. The truth in the old models of the ground of all being and the fountain of all life lies in the paradox that in the very costliness of creation, in the very act of his wearing himself out, he is at the same time renewed. Popular piety has rightly acclaimed him the Eternal One. Theologians have mistakenly interpreted that in which the eternality consists.

The costliest aspect of creation is letting the creatures be. It also provides the principal clue to the solution of the problem of evil. Evil, though fundamentally negative, is a terrible reality. It exhibits the price of the risk that God assumes when, in sending his creatures forth, he refrains from restricting them. That self-restraining love inevitably results in the struggle we see written into the entire realm we call Nature. That which oppresses us in our encounter with Nature is precisely that inevitable outcome of the divine permissiveness. The education of a creature that is given the scope God insists on bestowing on all his creatures is incalculably long and arduous. Nor is it by any means always successful. So one would expect: the stakes are high. Millions of creatures, including extinct species such as the mammoth and the dinosaur, have perished in the evolutionary process that has at length resulted in the emergence of that remarkable half-beast half-angel we call man. As the process unfolds we can see ever-increasing possibilities for good and evil, that is to say, a greater and greater spectrum of freedom. The greater the development of freedom, the more poignant the awareness of the necessity that is its correlative.

Origen's thought is provocative here, though one must be cautious in interpreting that most learned and audaciously imaginative of the early Fathers, for the text of many of his works has been lost and his teaching is probably traduced through simplistic reconstruction. Among the most widely recognized aspects of Origenism, however, is the view that creation itself is a kind of fall. This view has generally been taken to mean that the mere fact of our finitude is sufficient to throw us, so to speak, into the condition that traditional theologians have called original sin. That is not to say that the truth represented in the stories of the fall of Lucifer and the fall of Adam is to be set aside; but it does mean that to be a finite creature at all is to be somehow in a state that requires redemption.

Critics of Origen customarily point out that such a view fails to distinguish between finitude and sin. From a traditionalist standpoint that may well be so; but we should ask ourselves whether Origen may not have caught a glimpse of a truth elsewhere much overlooked, that to be a creature is to be left alone, that is, thrown into being with the need to discover and exercise freedom in the difficult environment of a community of other creatures at various stages of evolutionary development. A creature, when so thrown into existence, cannot be said to sin till he exercises his will in a negative way, that is, in a way contrary to the principles of the Being who is his creator; nevertheless, he is already, in his very coming-to-be as a finite creature, precipitated into a situation that is in itself tainted with negativity. Origen was unique among the ancient Fathers of the Church in teaching that the ultimate source of evil is to be found in a pre-mundane fall of equal created spirits who, slipping from the good state for which they were destined, became respectively angels, demons, and humans. In other words, what theologians call the fall of Adam took place in a spiritual, pre-natal existence.[9]

So then, not only is the story of the Garden of Eden to be interpreted allegorically, as Origen says;[10] the "fall" allegory is an allegory of the nature of creation itself. For what is Origen saying if not that in the very act of creation all creatures fall in some measure, since there is no way in which a creature can develop in such a way as to attain any destiny he may have simply by holding on, so to speak, to his pristine purity, as one tries to keep unstained an immaculately laundered shirt? To be a creature *is* to be "fallen," in the sense that a creature is "thrown," as Sartre has put it, into existence. There is no moral turpitude attached to one's being in this condition; yet it is a condition in which further falls are not only possible but, in view of the vastness of the universe, inevitable. Not only is humanity degenerate; even the "good" angels, simply in virtue of their finitude, share in some measure in the universal degeneracy of finite creatures. Whatever makes the angels so splendid must be something they have achieved rather than something they have preserved like a clean shirt. Origen's well-known doctrine of the pre-existence of the soul (a doctrine similar to but not identical with transmigration)[11] fits, of course, into that schema. What does *not* fit into it is the traditional model of a creation in the pastpreterite tense. Origen unequivocally teaches that crea-

---

[9] *Origen, De principiis,* ii, 8f.

[10] Ibid., iv, 3.

[11] Origen calls transmigration "foreign to the Church of God" and notes that it is "not anywhere set forth in the Scriptures." (See, e.g., his *Commentary on Matthew,* 13,1.) Nevertheless he is peculiarly interested in transmigratory notions. Though he does not allow metempsychosis in the old Pythagorean sense, he does hold that nothing spiritual can be destroyed, so he cannot regard death as a final decision on the soul's fate. The soul may turn into a devil or an angel in a process that goes on and on till the final Apocatastasis, when even Satan is to be saved.

tion is eternally ongoing. Though this notion has been traditionally outlawed on scriptural and other grounds, modern biblical scholars are nowadays much more cautious about condemning it for such reasons. At any rate, Origen's view on this question, whatever we may think of it, hints once again that in one way or another he may have grasped better than most of the Fathers the nature of divine Being. What we know of inconsistencies in Origen's thought, as exhibited in his extant work, suggests moreover that he was groping for a way of expressing what the Church, even with the help of the trinitarian language already in use in his time, had failed adequately to express about the nature of divine Being, whose omnipotence, Origen points out, is limited by his goodness and wisdom.[12]

I am not, of course, claiming that Origen's thought foreshadows anything like the kenotic view of Being I am presenting. I call attention to Origenism as an ancient element in Christian thought that may be more hospitable than are the more conventional formulations to a view such as, in our modern situation, I am advocating. Origen's interest for us lies in his openness to theological notions that make much more sense to anyone accustomed to a modern evolutionary understanding of the universe than do the traditional formulations. There can be no doubt at all that the importance of Origenism was for long obscured, especially in the West, by Augustine's condemnation of his views as heterodox and the weight of orthodox tradition against him in the Latin Church. In recent decades some scholars such as the Jesuit Cardinal Daniélou have shown afresh the enormous importance of Origen and the need, in face of centuries of misguided prejudice against him, to rehabilitate him in the light of modern knowledge.

The kind of logical dilemma presented in arguments of the Mackie-Flew type can arise only where theological

[12] *Contra Celsum*, 3.

categories have been first of all squeezed into the straight-jacket of a very latinized mode of thought. Once we are thoroughly inured to that style of thinking, there is no honest way out of the intellectual predicament into which the problem of evil forces us. Where, within that Latin mould, theologians do try to answer the objectors without sophistry, they do so by introducing, generally without explication and sometimes even unconsciously, an understanding of the character of divine omnipotence such as the one for which I have argued. Such an understanding cannot be presented without ado, however, as a normal or even legitimate interpretation of the traditional formulations about divine omnipotence. Therefore, however absurd the Mackie-Flew type of objection must always appear to the ordinarily intelligent, practicing Christian or observant Jew, it should be taken seriously if only because it exhibits the consequences of an uncritical acceptance of the traditional way of formulating the character of divine omnipotence as though it were the infinite exercise of a super-sultanic power, and of a radical failure to take seriously enough the theological proposition that God is love.

The master key to the unraveling of the puzzle lies in the insight that no jealousy can enter into the divine love. In creaturely love jealousy constitutes a component distorted by the fear of loss or annihilation. It causes us to interfere with other beings and impede them in one way or another. For every other being is in some respect my competitor. Therein lies the truth of Sartre's tortured assertion that "hell is other people." Even inanimate objects are potentially my rivals. I am jealous even of rocks and underbrush when they get in my way, impeding my access from one place to another. So I bulldoze them away to make myself a road. I may feel I have to compete with tall, beautiful trees for the air and sunshine I want, so I cut them down. I cannot let them be, for I see the situation as a case of my survival or theirs. My jealousy inhibits my love. Out of jealousy a man may kill his dearest friend. Christians have even been envious of other Christians, suspecting that God has favored these others more than he has favored them. Jealousy is the canker that enters into all creaturely relationships in the tooth-and-claw, dog-eat-dog universe in which we are set.

Half a millennium before the writer of the Johannine epistle proclaimed that God is love, Plato had already perceived the consequences of that absence of jealousy in God. "Let me tell you then," he makes Timaeus say to Socrates, "why the creator made this world of generation. He was good and the good can never have any jealousy of anything. And being free of jealousy he desired that all things should be as like himself as they could be. . . . God desired that all things should be good and nothing bad, so far as this was attainable." [13] Here the modern critic is inclined to object: "But why should not the complete elimination of the bad be achieved by an omnipotent creator?" The answer lies, I believe, in the recognition of three fundamental principles.

First, in the act of creation God's love is completely unhampered by jealousy since he has no possible ontic rivals. He can be under no temptation to limit his creatures in any way except in the bare fact of their creatureliness. He alone can love his creatures and let them be. But that means he does not create beings according to a hierarchy, limiting a being's possibilities to a certain range, as in Aristotle's system in which a tiger can never become any better than the finest of tigers or a dog than the finest of dogs: the finest, that is, of a creature's own species. Nor does God create angels and men and birds and vegetables: such a class distinction would be an imposed limitation on the creature. So all the specificity a creature can have when it issues from the Creator would seem to be that of creatureliness with the

[13] *Timaeus*, 30.

potentiality of unlimited growth within the creaturely order of being. To the creature is given the immense opportunity, together with the immense risk, of making his own way.

Second, in the act of creation God confers in some way his own nature upon all his creatures. That is what is expressed in the classic Christian doctrine of the *imago Dei*, according to which man is made in the divine image. If our first model is correct, however, the image of God must inhere in some measure in every creature at every stage of his development. Hence the profundity of the concept of reverence for life that is so familiar in Hinduism and that Schweitzer sought to teach the West. The image of God is only more noticeable, because more fully developed, in a human being than in a canary or a turnip. Man is engaged in a struggle to manifest more and more the nature of Being bequeathed to him in the act of divine creation. That view of human destiny need not entail the notion of divinization or deification, which according to scripture is at the heart of the temptation to go astray from our destiny. The creaturely possibilities beyond man are staggering enough within the creaturely order. For me to ask for more would be to deny the fundamental nature of Being, to lose myself in God when it is given to me to find myself in the full splendor of my creatureliness, of which the attainment of humanity has presumably given me only a faint foretaste. Hence the appositeness of the Lucifer myth: Lucifer, envious of God, wanted to become God, and in his rebellion sought to cause Adam and Eve to entertain similarly misguided ambitions.[14]

Third, if Being is in its fundamental character an outpouring of love, we must face the consequences of that astonishing affirmation of Christian faith. Since the root

[14] The Qur'ān (sūra XX, 116) introduces in this connection an interesting mythos: at the creation of man, God enjoined the angels to prostrate themselves before Adam; but Lucifer refused. That story, too, might be interpreted as expressing the central element of jealousy as the impediment to every creature's growth. Jealousy of another creature was the downfall of the highest of the angels.

metaphor is love, the other dependent metaphors cannot be used apart from it. The only kind of wisdom God can exhibit must be whatever kind is compatible with his love. The only kind of knowledge he can be said to have is the kind that springs from love. That is, he may be said, indeed, as the Bible has it, to know when a little sparrow falls to the ground; but the divine omnipotence would not be affected by his not knowing all the numbers in the New York telephone directory. Likewise, the only kind of power that God can intelligibly be said to exercise is whatever power love can be said to exercise. As God is incapable of any envy, so he is incapable of wantonness. Having no "worlds to conquer," no possible "ambition" (if one may so speak), he can, as we have already seen, go only one way, the way of self-diminishment, which is the way of love. So he comes in meekness because he *is* meek, in humility because he *is* humble. Yet that meekness, that humility, is the greatest possible moral splendor and the greatest of all power.

When we take these three points into account, the evil in the universe is seen in a light that makes the standard critical objections irrelevant. For we are no longer to be seen as the puppets of a monstrous deity giving and withholding according to his whim, or as a deity hidebound by his own "rational" nature. We can no longer think of ourselves as having been accorded a measure of free choice such as an experimenter accords to a rat in a laboratory maze. On the contrary, the divine act of creation bestows on every creature an unlimited potentiality for development. At first the creature, being not even sentient, cannot exercise any freedom at all; yet in the course of time life emerges and eventually intelligence. The development is against incalculable odds: therein lies its value. Furthermore, it is tenuously held. We do not carry it in a shatterproof box but, as Paul says of the Christian's treasure, "in earthen vessels." Presumably the struggle is intensified as evolution proceeds: the fiercest battle, as Paul also notes,

is not against mere flesh and blood but against wickedness
in the higher dimensions of finite being.

John Stuart Mill, a well-known nineteenth-century critic
of the traditional notion of divine omnipotence, unexpectedly helps us to clear up the misunderstanding, more
radical than he could have suspected, about what divine
creative power is. He points out that "every indication of
Design in the Kosmos is so much evidence against the
Omnipotence of the Designer. For what is meant by
Design? Contrivance: the adaptation of means to an end.
But the necessity for contrivance—the need for employing
means—is a consequence of the limitation of power.
Wisdom and contrivance are shown in overcoming difficulties, and there is no room for them in a Being for whom no
difficulties exist." [15] Mill, a proponent of the view that God's
power is limited by conditions not of his own choosing, is
assuming no less than do many traditionalist theologians
that divine power is an ordaining and controlling, an
executive and administrative, kind of power. On the basis of
that primitive understanding of the character of divine
omnipotence, of course Mill is right, and he makes his point
tellingly. Evidence for design, far from being the proof of
the existence of a divine Being that it has been traditionally
taken to be, is really evidence *against* the existence of such
a Being, when that Being is conceived, in the typical
primitive fashion, as the supreme magician, who in creating
need but utter the magic spell or wave the wizard's wand.
As God says *fiat lux et facta est lux* ("let there be light, and
there was light"), so he should be able to say "let there be
men" with similarly instant results. But then one must ask,
why stop at humanity? Why not "let there be supermen"?
And then must come the inevitable question: Why the
divine stinginess in creating a hierarchy of creatures when

[15] John Stuart Mill, *Three Essays on Religion*, Part II, in *Essays on Ethics,
Religion and Society: Collected Works of John Stuart Mill*, Vol. X, ed. J. M. Robson
(Toronto: University of Toronto Press, 1969), p. 451.

omnipotence could have ordained all creatures instantly the highest and best?

When the mind works with such a magical model it properly revolts against even the slightest *soupçon* of divine planning or contrivance or design. A competent magician needs a minimum of equipment: an omnicompetent one should need none at all. In the Arabian Nights one can travel by magic; but one needs the assistance of a carpet: Why should God need even the carpet? We recall the ancient objection: why should Zeus need even nod?

Hume had similarly misunderstood the character of divine benevolence when he asked: "In short, might not the Deity exterminate all ill, wherever it were to be found; and produce all good, without any preparation or long progress of causes and effects?" [16] The demand, then, is not only for magical power; it is also for a no less magical instant goodness.

Christians have often been to blame for engendering these gross misconceptions that have become, through Hume's legacy, standard pabulum in modern philosophical critique. Through caricature of the trinitarian formula and of the doctrine of the Incarnation, popular piety bequeathed to philosophers a fundamentally false notion of the Christian God. Few Christian divines in the earlier part of our own century can have more trenchantly expressed the situation than did Streeter when he wrote more than sixty years ago, in a paper entitled "The Suffering of God":

Men still spoke of the love of God: they only really meant it when they thought of God, the Son; clemency at most—a royal prerogative—was imagined of the Father. . . . The Christian *Creed* acknowledges but one God and one quality of Godhead —so far Athanasius won his cause; but the Christian *imagination* has been driven by this postulate of the impassibility of

[16] David Hume, *Dialogues Concerning Natural Religion*, XI, in C. W. Hendel, Jr., *Hume Selections* (New York: Charles Scribner's Sons, 1927), p. 374.

God to worship two. Side by side sit throned in heaven God the Father, omnipotent, unchangeable, impassible, and on his right hand God the Son, *"passus, crucifixus, mortuus, resurrectus."* What is this but Arianism, routed in the field of intellectual definition, triumphing in the more important sphere of the imaginative presentation of the object of the belief? [17]

Perhaps, however, the blame should not be laid entirely at the door of popular piety, for the theologians, while they embodied the Athanasian formula in the Church's creeds, were themselves under the joint influence of Hebrew and Greek thought, which had unwittingly conspired together in bequeathing to the Church the metaphysical presupposition of an impassible God.[18]

There lies the root of our gravest difficulties with the concept of evil. We have rarely taken seriously enough the supreme biblical testimony about the character of God: *ho theos agapē estin*, God is love. The case I have been arguing, far from doing injury to the concept of divine omnipotence, exalts it as a kenotic almightiness. What then remains of the problem of evil turns into a question about the nature of freedom and the necessity of the struggle entailed in its development. The reality of that freedom and of that necessity in Nature confronts us daily. Nothing that we know in Nature seems to achieve its status without struggle. Development, whether of life or of mind, is a succession of prison-breaks.

At first the qualities needed for success seem to be assertiveness and aggression; but as the development proceeds these "jungle" qualities are no longer sufficient; nor, indeed, are they even relevant to our condition. As the transition from war to peace proceeds, we tend to expect

---

[17] B. J. Streeter, "The Suffering of God," in *Hibbert Journal*, 1914.

[18] For a valuable survey of Christian thought on the impassibility of God, see J. K. Mozley, *The Impassibility of God* (Cambridge: Cambridge University Press, 1926), already quoted in Chapter V.

that the struggle should abate. The more vigorous among us may even regret what seems to be the passing of the old martial virtues and the dreary prospect of a morally flabby enjoyment of life in which even the life of the mind turns into the enjoyment of clever games rather than to engagement in intellectual enterprise. It looks as though survival would become easier yet at the same time less worthwhile in such a dull, ambitionless world. In fact, however, the case is very different. For as we move into a society in which the individual has to adjust his way of life and his mode of thinking to a more highly organized and "packed together" society, he discovers sooner or later that the key to survival lies not in the old kind of moral fibre he had been accustomed to cultivate in order to survive in a tooth-and-claw jungle, but, rather, in a new range of virtues. He sees now that his hope lies not in spreading himself by trampling on his foes; it lies, rather, in a recessionary program in which self-humbling, self-diminishment, even self-sacrifice, provide ways of survival.

> *Behold the door to heaven is set so low*
> *That he must learn to stoop who in would go.*

In learning to renounce the follies of tooth-and-claw aggression we begin to apprehend the secret of divine power, the power that is in the structure and at the core of Being.

Yet while such a view should clarify our understanding of the character of the power that is at the heart of all things and raises the whole mystery of evil up to a different level, the puzzle of the irrational disproportionateness of evil remains. Not only do the vast emptinesses of the universe seem unrelated to the kind of Being and the kind of agapistic power we have been considering; the kinds of accident and tragedy that occur seem to stand apart from the vision I have presented of the gradual unfolding of the divine power of self-abnegation through the struggle and anguish of evolutionary development. A herd of wild elephants will not only trample a man to death; it is as likely to trample to death an Albert Schweitzer as a Charles Manson. Indeed, the animal cunning to be found in the lowest sort of men tends to be lost as men open themselves to, and make their own, the love of God. The finer the man, the more unprotected he seems in the jungle.

Are not we back, then, to the old question of Job and countless others? Where is the divine power, however understood, when we see the very generosity of the great and good man expose him to disaster, while the brutal savage, by his low cunning, walks away from it with a cruel grin on his bestial face? Take a macabre example: the man who gallantly plunges in the water to try to save a drowning child is accorded a hero's funeral; but in the background leeringly skulks the hero's lifelong rival, a stronger swimmer who might have saved the child but who, having preferred discretion to valor, now sits smugly gloating over his own survival and the downfall of his rival. Who has won? It is all very well to say "I'd rather be the corpse than such a louse" or "it will do the skunk no good in the long run." The fact remains that the corpse is a corpse and the skunk a living man. For the case is really much worse than Job has it. The wicked do not merely prosper and the righteous merely suffer; the wicked live while the righteous die. And all Christians know that at the heart of their faith is the case of the most righteous One of all who not only died in the prime of life but died in the greatest agony and shame—a shame augmented by the fact that thousands upon thousands of cruel men and women have since successfully used him as a cloak for their own self-seeking.

The answer to the mystery of evil is made clearer by an understanding of the character of divine power; but the mystery is by no means entirely resolved. Evil in all its hideous, barbaric might seems to prevail. Is not this evidence of the ultimate godlessness of the universe? No, it is merely evidence of a deep-seated presupposition that there should be someone-in-charge to guarantee the triumph of justice at every point. Why should there be such a guarantor of justice? How could there be, with impunity to our freedom? We have no right to expect anything of the sort. Indeed, if we had, the rocks would reverently curtsy in the presence of life and the mountains bow low at the emergence of mind; but on the contrary they have sat smugly through Bethlehem and Calvary, more unmoved than the crudest cursing soldier, more unrelenting than the most ruthless of despots.

If, however, Christianity teaches any doctrine at all, it is that the anguish we feel in that picture is by no means only a creaturely anguish. It is *a fortiori* the anguish of God. Likewise, the sense of the absence of God, a familiar trial in the life of every Christian, for which the *locus classicus* is the cry of dereliction on the Cross, *Eli, Eli, lama sabach-thani,* has its counterpart in God himself. For a creature to withdraw from God as we creatures do must surely be infinite agony for him who is the God of love. Confronted with the sphinx-like face of what we call Nature, man is disposed to see evil as all-pervasive, all-victorious, and the meaninglessness of the panorama is mirrored in his own aching heart; but, if God is indeed as we have depicted him, he too must know the pain of seeing the millions of creatures who absent themselves from *him*. The profound truth of this is dramatically presented in the Catholic devotion to the Sacred Heart. Evil is the failure of creatures to respond to the love of God that is the law of their own being. That failure, which surrounds us in Nature, plagues us at every point by providing obstacles to our own growth in kenotic Being. God, who can have no need to grow, cannot be so plagued; yet because he is so completely He-who-loves his anguish at the lovelessness of his creatures must be all the more poignant.

The divine permissiveness that lets all creatures be can help us to understand how evil emerges and what it is; but grave indeed would be our misunderstanding of the God-is-love affirmation, and feeble would be our attempt to solve the problem of evil, if we were to go no further. Nothing that has been said about love and sacrifice, about struggle and freedom, about creativity and divine permissiveness, can exhibit the character of kenotic power or provide an adequate clarification of the mystery of evil until we take account of the place of providence and prayer. To that final aspect of kenotic power our next chapter will be devoted.

CHAPTER IX

Providence and Prayer

He prayeth best who loveth best
All things both great and small.

—S. T. Coleridge, *The Ancient Mariner*

To the casual, skeptical onlooker, nothing seems more incongruous than the combination of what he takes to be the Christian doctrine of God and what he sees to be the Christian practice of prayer. According to traditional doctrine, God knows everything, and everything is in the last resort determined by his beneficent yet inexorable will. Could anything, then, be sillier than the spectacle of men and women asking him to intervene at their behest to change the course of events or avert a personal danger? As C. S. Lewis liked to remind us, God is a father, not a senile uncle.

The average, moderately intelligent and informed observer finds such petitionary prayer worse than the primitive worship of the savage who pleads with and threatens his gods when they do not send rain, and even beats his idol in hope of shaking the rain out of him. For while the savage, having no satisfactory systematic theology, could know no better, the Christian claims to have a dogmatic revelation that seems clearly to exclude and make ridiculous the notion of asking God to change his mind or of suggesting to him a better way of dealing with Aunt Jennifer's ingrowing toenail. Devout Christians, indeed, following the example of Jesus in the Garden of Gethsemane, conclude their prayers with words such as "but when all that is said, Lord, I want your will to prevail, not mine." But if so, why the prayer? Is it not at best merely an elegant way of saying something such as a boy might say to his father: "I'd really like a new car; but if you don't care to give me one, it's all right. I don't want to break with you over a thing like that."

The comparison is, of course, intentionally outrageous. I am using it to exhibit the incompatibility of traditional Christian thought and traditional Christian practice. Devout Christians are, as a rule, better at praying than they are at thinking. Nevertheless, to the thoughtful Christian, the only kinds of prayer that make any sense at all in view of traditional theological formulations would seem to be prayers of adoration, praise, and thanksgiving, that is, prayers that acknowledge the state of affairs ordained by God. In prayers of that kind Christians adore, praise and thank God that such is indeed the state of affairs. Such prayer is easy to justify. To the objection that God does not need the thanksgiving or the praise, one replies that indeed he does not but that nevertheless God recognizes that a loving heart will always give such praise as surely as a lively child will always shout and jump. It is therefore "right and good" that a Christian should give it. Petitionary prayer is in a very different case. So also, indeed, is intercessory prayer. A distinction is customarily made between petitionary prayer, in which we ask for specific favors, and intercessory prayer, in which we pray for other people, that they may be restored to health, for example, or be enabled to come to a right decision. Yet while intercessory prayer may be commended as more altruistic than is typical petitionary prayer, neither kind fits the traditional concept of God.

That is, of course, as we should now see clearly enough,

because traditional formulations and modes of conceptualizing God have severely distorted what Christians know at heart must be the case and what is to be found in the most characteristic message of the Bible: God is love. Once we see that God really enters into the scene of our sufferings, our failures, and even our sins, though he refrains from interfering with our response and our actions, the function of all prayer becomes far more intelligible. For then one may see easily enough that while God refrains from interference, he is also ready to provide help when asked. "Behold, I stand at the door and knock; if anyone hears my voice and opens the door, I will come in to him and eat with him, and he with me." [1] Providence awaits prayer.

Christians have been generally uneasy, however, about the whole question of petitionary and intercessory prayer, and their uneasiness reflects an uneasiness about their concept of God. A telling example is provided by Bishop Gore, who nearly a hundred years ago chided Rome for its encouragement of Marian devotion. He quotes a passage from Liguori's *Glories of Mary* [2] that proposes to call Mary the Queen of Mercy and Christ the King of Justice and suggests that while one must expect a king to maintain justice one may look to a good queen for unlimited compassion. [3] We have already noted much earlier that Yves Congar has critically treated that same theme in a now more ecumenical climate of thought, showing that a false christology had deprived popular medieval devotion of the humanity of Christ so that a Mediatrix had to take the place of the Mediator.

There is no doubt that the Reformation was a corrective against excessive reliance on Mary as the only practical

[1] Rev. 3:20 (RSV).

[2] Alfonso dei Liguori (1696–1787), founder of the Redemptorists. In the history of moral theology in the Roman Church after Trent he was extremely influential.

[3] Charles Gore, *The Incarnation of the Son of God*, Bampton Lectures, 1891 (London: John Murray, 1892), 2nd ed., p. 3; and Appendix, note 2, p. 233.

source of mercy. We may well ask, however, whether a perhaps even more dangerous distortion may not have occurred, in popular Protestant devotion, through a dichotomy between the just Father and the merciful Son. People have felt that when it is a question of adoring and praising God, the prayers may be properly addressed to the Father, but when a supplicant seeks mercy and compassion the prayer should be addressed to the Son. If one should be so bold as to address a prayer for forgiveness to the Father, at least it should always be very specifically made *through* the Son and the clemency asked for his sake. I do not think I caricature the situation by suggesting that one could almost translate the *Salve Regina* into a hymn that many Protestants would find fairly congenial, if one were simply to transfer the address from the Mother to the Son and conclude by asking that, after this life, the Son might show us the Father. Yet of course only because of a highly artificial, not to say tritheistic, understanding of God, in which the Father is seen as unbending and implacable while the Son is compassionate and kind, could that sort of attitude be maintained.

All that suggests a grave departure in popular tradition, Catholic and Protestant, from the affirmation that God is love. It is that departure that makes a rationale for petitionary prayer seem so difficult to find. The writer of the first letter of John, in which occurs the basic affirmation "God is love," presented future generations of Christians with a puzzle wherein he also said that "we have an advocate with the Father, Jesus Christ the righteous." [4] If one needs an advocate, it is easy to see how natural it would become to the average person to look for the advocacy in a purely human being rather than in one who, the Church officially proclaimed, is both fully human and fully divine. But if God is love, why should one need an advocate at all?

[4] I John 2:1.

One needs an advocate to plead with a just judge in order that he may be persuaded to be as clement as possible in the administration of justice. For clemency does not belong to a judge's nature or function; it is only something of which he is capable. To appeal for the intervention of an advocate in approaching one whose fundamental nature is love is plainly to lack confidence in the love. The Reformers, in seeing the unsatisfactoriness of this, showed a sure theological instinct.

The Reformers' practical instinct, however, may have been less sure. The prohibition of Mary to the people had to result in the development either of a lame-duck sort of tritheism or else of the notion that Christ, whom the Middle Ages had de-humanized, must be quickly re-humanized by de-divinizing him. The root of the trouble was not, as modern secular humanists tend to suppose, an excessive preoccupation with theology. On the contrary, it may be attributed to a failure or an inability to probe radically enough to go below the doctrine of the Trinity to the truth the formulation had been designed to express.

When one does take seriously the "God is love" motif, the whole philosophy of Christian worship is at once radically affected. For then, as we have seen, the letting-be of creative Being entails the suffering of God, because wherever creatures fail to attain their full stature, wherever "creation groaneth and travaileth in pain together," [5] God enters into and endures that pain, the poignancy of which consists above all in his renunciation of all interference, all compulsion, all external restraint. As Professor Moule has eloquently put it in terms of christology: "*Kenōsis* actually is *plerōsis;* which means that the human limitations of Jesus are seen as a positive expression of his divinity rather than as a curtailment of it: 'Jesus divinest when thou most art man.' " [6] Devotionally this means that one may indeed ask

[5] Rom. 8:22.

[6] C. F. D. Moule, "The Manhood of Jesus in the New Testament," quoted by

whatever one wants to ask, so long as that which is asked is not incompatible with the kenotic nature of Being itself.

To ask anything of God in prayer is to invoke the Providence of God. It is to ask that circumstances or events be arranged differently from the way in which they might be arranged. It is to ask, in some sense, for divine intervention. Providence, when conceived in traditional terms, cannot but look like divine interference, not to say tinkering. When, however, we see God as *always* entering into and suffering with his creatures, Providence, though not indeed unmysterious, becomes much more intelligible. For to see the working of Providence in human events is to see that God, in response to prayer, has found a way to do what seemed undoable. The saying "love will find a way" is, indeed, a popular expression of a fundamental truth about divine Being. The way God finds and discloses is not available *to me* until I seek its disclosure in prayer. A hundred doors may stand wide open to me; but if I suffer from a spiritual glaucoma that obscures my peripheral vision I may see only the one door that is closed. The model of Providence I am proposing here excludes any notion of divine intervention of such kind as would seem to make God an errand-boy, either to carry out our whims for us or to actualize for us our ideals. The task and the responsibility remain ours; nor does God change anything or do anything in our stead; nevertheless (I am suggesting) he, being already in the "dead-end" situation with us, does show us ways of coping and sustains us in our efforts to cope. So prayers such as the familiar *Domine, labia mea aperies,* "O Lord, open thou my lips," and *Deus in adjutorium meum intende,* "O God, make speed to save me" are paradigmatic of all petitionary prayer. We do not ask that God ghostwrite our speeches while we laze in the sun; we ask for what is less yet more than that, namely, that he be with us in our

J. A. T. Robinson, *The Human Face of God* (Philadelphia: Westminster Press, 1973), p. 208.

struggle to write or speak or travel or solve puzzles or dig ditches.

Here one may well object: That is all very fine, but how does it help me if I have leukemia and want to live? For it seems plain that in such circumstances only a "good old-fashioned miracle" can possibly help me. Now, of course, it might be that at the moment of my prayer the medical researchers came along with the long-awaited cure for that disease, just in time for me to be among the first to benefit. To *expect* any such result from prayer is, however, fundamentally irreligious and due to a misunderstanding of the nature and function both of Providence and of prayer.

Misunderstanding inevitably results from attitudes that presuppose a set of "natural rights" for man. So long as we harbor such presuppositions, we shall seem to be at once so much in the grip of injustice and so much flung to the winds of chance that the whole notion of divine Providence will look like a bad joke. I take the Christian view to be, rather, that we have no rights at all, only duties, and our first duty is, as I suggested at the outset, thankfulness for life itself. As we might say colloquially, all else is "gravy." If I have grounds for complaint in the court of heaven because I am poor or lame, what a parade of suits might be taken there by trillions of what was once called "the lower creation." Would not my dog, were he not so ignorant, have plenty of cause for complaint that he was born subhuman? True, he is healthy and handsome; but might not he well deem it better to be an undistinguished and plebeian human, perhaps even a poor and crippled human, rather than the finest prize-winning Airedale? What man or woman, lamenting his or her slow wit or plain looks, would prefer to be, say, a handsome and nimble salmon or trout?

There is, in short, no creature that might not grumble at his lack of "endowment" or have no cause to envy another. Everything living on this planet other than man might well envy the extraordinary privilege we enjoy of being human. When we ask Providence "to come to our aid," then, we dare ask only for help in directing us to opportunities we have overlooked. Even to have a short human life of childhood poverty ending in death from leukemia at the age of twenty would seem infinitely better than dying of old age as a healthy beetle or well-fed worm.

That prayer is psychologically therapeutic for the supplicant, benefiting him independently of any benefit that may come to those for whom his supplications are asked, has been long widely recognized. Dr. Alexis Carrel, a highly original though much criticized thinker who won the Nobel Prize for his work on suturing blood vessels and further recognition for his work on cancer research, was quite definite in his medical opinion of the efficacy of prayer. He called it "the most powerful form of energy that one can generate," and he claimed that "its influence on the human mind and body is as demonstrable as that of secreting glands."

The importance of the notion, however, lies far deeper than can be expressed in psychological terms. Prayer, uttered in anguish and sincerity of heart, opens the supplicant to the direct influence of him who is self-abnegating *par excellence,* and in doing so makes accessible the "other doors" that only sacrificial love can see. Of course my prayer is futile if I expect God to work a miracle for my sick brother while I, having done my canonical duty, forget the whole thing and go off to the beach. If I pray well, however, I shall learn through my prayer how best to help my brother by putting my action where my mouth is. My brother, the object of my prayers, is helped by my action; but he is also supported in his trouble by the knowledge that others are praying for him. That support might be merely the psychological crutch to which Charles Schultz's beloved cartoon character Charlie Brown refers in his characteristic epigram: "Security is knowing you are not

alone." The support my brother receives may issue, however, from a change in the relationship with God that he
sees through the action in and consequent upon my prayer.
That is to say, through my prayer he, too, may be shown the
nature of Being and, through openness to its source, find his
own road to victory. What ensues upon that, he will rightly
call providential.

For that is what prayer and Providence are about. The
solutions to our problems are around us. It is we who,
because of our false understanding of the nature of Being,
seek to solve them in impossible ways. To be so foolish as to
ask God to intercept a bullet, suspending it in mid-air in the
course of its trajectory would be, of course, asking the
impossible. Every cartoonist who uses such a notion as a
joke sees, in one way or another, that it is a joke precisely
because of the meaningless incongruity in it. The meaningless incongruity springs from bad theology. For an under-
graduate to ask God to get him a *magna* when he hasn't
done even enough work for a pass is of a similar order. The
case of the woman who, having just administered her
husband a lethal dose of prussic acid, instantly repents and
prays that it may turn into lemonade before reaching his
gastro-intestinal tract, would differ only in being more
macabre. Such prayers are foolish at best and blasphemous
at worst, not because they exaggerate the power of God but
because they dictate methods to God, who, if he is in the
least as he is biblically depicted, must have at his disposal,
when we earnestly call for providential intervention, both
better methods and better means. In the picturesque
language of the Bible, he has in readiness for such purposes
twelve legions of angels,[7] that is, messengers of his infinitely
powerful and surprising *agapē*.

Providence awaits, however, not only our prayer but the
use to which we put our prayer. The instant result of good

[7] Matt. 26:53.

prayer is, as Carrel and others have so clearly seen, therapeutic. My mind is clarified and my energies set free; but unless my vision is also redirected in openness to God and my will steeled for action to put my deeds where my vision is, the only result I can know will be exactly what the psychotherapists tell us it is: a clarified mind and a liberated energy. That, however beneficial, is far indeed from exhausting the power of prayer in appropriating the methods and the means that Providence ever stands ready to make available to us.

Everyone who is in the way of taking life seriously at all is familiar with the experience Sartre has dramatized in *Huis clos*. No way! Look where you will, turn as you may, you have reached a dead end. Prayer will make no difference to that, nor can Providence intervene, for there is nothing to intervene about. Nevertheless, earnest prayer can so clear the vision as to show us, alongside the *huis clos*, a hundred *ouvertures* from the side alleys that lead out of the darkness of our today's prison into the marvellous light of tomorrow's meadows. But we must learn that prayer makes no *huis clos* into a *huis ouvert*. Its function is more remarkable: to make us aware of better doors into unimaginably more exciting new pastures.

When, looking back on a chapter of our lives, we say, either with deep devotion or half-hearted piety, that such and such an event was providential, what do we mean? Surely we do not mean that the course of history was interrupted or reversed, as in a literalistic reading of the story recorded by Deutero-Isaiah, according to which the shadow cast by the sun on a stairway "went back ten steps on the stairway down which it had gone." [8] Nor could we mean that when, according to all the laws of physics and aeronautics, I should have been killed in an air crash, I was inexplicably found safe and healthy in my seat looking on at

[8] Isa. 38:8 (NEB).

the mangled corpses all around me. I might well mean, however, that, having carefully planned a certain flight, I had made reservations for it and had been so set on catching it that the unexpected appearance of half a dozen obstacles in my way only strengthened my resolve till at length, in my fierce determination to catch that plane, I fell down the escalator and broke my femur, forcing me to go to hospital where, an hour later, I was to hear of the crash in which there was not a single survivor. Were I in the least disposed to see the hand of Providence in human affairs, I might indeed see it in the escape I would call providential. I might even see it as an answer, however oblique, to a prayer I had uttered that no harm might overtake me on whom my family depended so much for care and protection. Of course the accident harmed me, no doubt incapacitating me for several months; nevertheless that harm would have been remediable, not final.

Yet in no way, of course, could I ever provide anyone with demonstrative, assent-compelling proof of providential intervention. Indeed, it is precisely because the hand of God is seen under such guises, when it is seen at all, that the assertions of religious people are in the nature of the case unfalsifiable. Were they otherwise they would have to be the ostentatious intrusion of a despotic deity parading his power with arrogant *panache*, not the quiet intervention of the One who hides his agapistic power with the modesty peculiar to self-sacrificial love.

Much popular misunderstanding of the workings of Providence and of the power of prayer lie in a persistent and false notion, namely, the notion that having freedom of choice is incompatible with belief in a providential God. There is no incompatibility. On the contrary, not till I have seen what the exercise of freedom really means to me and does for me do I begin to understand something of the nature of the God-who-loves, and not till I have caught a glimpse of the awful holiness of God's love do I begin to understand the meaning of human freedom. The two concepts are so much a part of each other that only the limitations of human thought require them to be theoretically separated. That artificial, theoretical separation of them grievously distorts for many people the nature of the reality to which respectively they point.

The truth of what I have just been saying is demonstrable to those accustomed to be puzzled by the disputes about the relation of morality to religion. The more we address ourselves to the intellectual study of religion and of ethics, the more we are forced to recognize that neither can give up the autonomy each claims. That is why everyone who knows anything of the nature of religion sees at once instinctively that when, more than a hundred years ago, Matthew Arnold defined religion as "morality touched with emotion," he was not only offering a non-definition, since the emotion tinging morality must be specifically religious emotion, thus emptying the definition of meaning; he was suggesting a connection between morality and religion that would destroy the value of both. With equally justified distaste would a moralist greet the notion that morality is but religion embodied in practice. Both such proposals are wrong and misleading because, in failing to recognize the sharp distinction between morality and religion, they obscure the character of both as surely as one would obscure the meaning of transcendence and immanence if one tried to understand them apart from one another and not as the correlative terms they are. The love of God enters into my will only when it can do so without even in the slightest degree diminishing or restricting my freedom, while my freedom cannot be realized except to the extent that I cease erecting self-assertive impediments to the entry of the self-limiting God into my life.

That we are able to erect impediments to the entry of God is exceedingly familiar in Christian experience. No Christian would see any objection to the statement, "God cannot forgive an impenitent sinner." For as we read in the Gospels that the sinful woman's "great love proves that her many sins have been forgiven," we learn also that "where little has been forgiven, little love is shown." [9] The presence of love is proof of forgiveness as the experience of forgiveness is proof of love. The absence of the one likewise exhibits the absence of the other. Why? Because so long as I choose to erect and sustain an impediment to God he will not intrude and so I must remain unforgiven. Where anger, hatred, or resentment, for instance, are present, they erect an impediment to the efficacy of prayer and the intervention of Providence. The power of the divine love cannot flow into nothing. We must be at least in some measure ready with our empty pitchers to receive the creative power he can bestow. Every grudge, every envy, every jealousy hinders what prayer can accomplish, because it blocks out the God who so respects us that, though (to use a picturesque symbol) his heart break a thousand times, he will not intrude.

Yet when all that is said, we have to reckon with the universal testimony of Christian experience that, when God is believed to intervene providentially at all, he always intervenes "exceeding abundantly above all that we ask or think, according to the power that worketh in us." [10] That is to say, the Christian, when he believes he discerns the workings of Providence, sees, not an occasional wand-waving from the hand of an omnipotent magician, but the infinitely ingenious because infinitely creative power of "the only wise God our Savior." [11]

We began our study by questioning the implication of the biblical phrase: "God is love." What kind of Providence is to be expected of him who is recognized in that affirmation?

[9] Luke 7:47 (NEB).
[10] Eph. 3:20.
[11] Jude 25.

It could be that, in the course of biological evolution and the ensuing development in the mind of man that may be called evolution, God simply stands by, awaiting opportunities to make passably good processes into better ones. There could be nothing in all God's creation that would fit neatly into the systematic theodicy of a Leibniz or (as Kierkegaard so clearly saw) into the all-encompassing metaphysic of a Hegel. God does not create and then re-enter a little while later with a program of redemption. All that is created is created for redemption, and the process, far from being smooth and systematic, is as terrible as is the love of God that is ever engaged in the redemption of all that has been called into existence.

In the early decades of our troubled century, the Great War, as it was called, brought about a carnage from which Europe has never fully recovered. In the midst of that awful holocaust, an English Congregationalist divine, P. T. Forsyth, reminded his hearers that they were still intoxicated by the facile notion of a steady evolutionary progress. He was indeed right. Even those who, like Fiske and Drummond, Savage and McCosh, were spiritualizing Darwin's biological discoveries, were inclined to see in the process a long series of steady steps inevitably leading from the low to the high, from ignorance to knowledge, from evil to good. When people theorize about such things they tend to see only the successes, which then appear as an orderly procession. In reading the history of science we are much prone to such a temptation. The working scientist is not, for he knows only too well what dreary valleys, strewn with failures, lie between the exhilarating little hills of his success. For those who engage in theological speculation, the hazard is certainly no less.

The notion of an evolutionary development within the creative purposes of God is ancient. There is a long, though special tradition about it, from Irenaeus in the second century of the Christian era to Pierre Teilhard de Chardin in our own. Forsyth, in addressing a cultivated audience in the midst of the war-shattered world of his day, was criticizing that tradition from within its own framework. I suspect that the critique of that prophetic thinker may be no less relevant to our condition today than it was when that brutal war was taking an optimistic and self-confident Western world by surprise. I therefore quote Forsyth's dramatic warning:

> What is it that would justify God to you? You have grown up in an age that has not yet got over the delight of having discovered in evolution the key to creation. You saw the long expanding series broadening to the perfect day. You saw it foreshortened in the long perspective, peak rising on peak, each successively catching the ascending sun. The dark valley, antres vast, and deserts horrible, you did not see. They were crumpled in the tract of time, and folded away from sight. The roaring rivers and thunders, the convulsions and voices, the awful conflicts latent in nature's ascent and man's—you could pass these over in the sweep of your glance. . . . But now you have been flung into one of these awful valleys. You taste what it has cost, thousands of times over, to pass from range to range of those illuminated heights. You are in bloody, monstrous, and deadly dark. . . . The air is as red as the rains of hell.[12]

In the Christian experience of Providence we catch only glimpses of what we believe to be its ever-present working. The Christian, in appropriating the redemptive fruits of the humiliation of Christ, discerns in an incomparably vivid way the meaning of the proposition "God is love." Yet we are too ready to detach the meaning of that supreme event from the nature of Being. Hence we tend too much to see Providence as God-with-gloves-on, and prayer as supplication to One seated on the velvet cushion of the Throne of

---

[12] P. T. Forsyth, *The Justification of God* (London: Latimer House, Ltd., 1948), p. 159. Forsyth's lectures, when originally published in 1917, bore the subtitle, *Lectures for War-Time on a Christian Theodicy.*

Heaven. If God is love he can never be properly symbolized as sitting down or holding up but always as on the move. His chase may sometimes seem as unhurried and his pace as unperturbed as Francis Thompson so beautifully describes;[13] but perhaps even that model is too redolent of our infatuation with immobility to do justice to the God who is called love. There was nothing unhurried about Mary's search for lodging in Bethlehem; nor was the Way of the Cross unperturbed.

Nor indeed is any human agony beautiful at close quarters, however it may look on an elegant Christmas card. The workings of love are not smooth or suave or sedate; they are anguished, awkward, incongruous. But above all they have within them the seed of the splendor of victory, for if God is love there can be, even in the most awkward squeezing of himself through the narrow slits of our impoverishment, no point at which he is not omni-victorious in the anguish of his self-attenuation. So to be surprised by a joy far beyond what we could ever by ourselves generate or sustain is to know God as surely as he can be known in this our very fleeting life in which we are all "running forward to death."[14]

---

[13] Francis Thompson, *The Hound of Heaven.*

[14] Heidegger's phrase is *Vorlaufen zum Tode;* see his *Sein und Zeit* (Tübingen: Neomarius Verlag, 1949), p. 267. In a race a *Vorlauf* is a running start. Heidegger's phrase suggests a leaping forward ahead of oneself, a very Nietzschean notion and conspicuously alien from the traditional ideal of serene participation in impassible Being.

CHAPTER X

A New Vision of the Self-Emptying God

On God's part creation is not an act of self-expansion but of restraint and re-nunciation.

—*Simone Weil, Waiting on God*

WE are now in a position to review the implications of the understanding of God that I have proposed in the foregoing study and to make possible a new vision of God as self-emptying Being.

Dynamism, the idolatry of power, which characterized primitive religion, has persisted in the monotheistic tradition, sometimes even becoming what we may call, by way of a useful neologism, "dynamolatry" (the worst form idolatry can take), to the great detriment of an authentic appreciation of God's nature. It has even obscured the special insights that this tradition has so usefully provided and enjoyed. We have seen that, although the doctrine of the Trinity furnished a model that alleviated some of the effects of a preoccupation with power that persisted in Christian modes of conceptualizing God, it can nevertheless act, and

often does act, as a buttress for the old power worship. I am
convinced that we must learn to revolutionize our thinking
about God in such a way that the old models of power-
worship are thoroughly undermined so that they may give
place to a radically new vision of God. "Giving place" is,
indeed, as we have seen, the one way in which we can "be
like God."

The worship of power is a natural starting-place for
religion. Who in a tribal village can command most
attention and respect? Certainly not the weakest member,
the one who can least defend the tribe against its enemies,
the one who is most impotent in the conservation of
whatever the tribe values and is the greatest drag on its
resources. No, of course the biggest and strongest acquires
prestige simply in virtue of his qualities of size and strength.
Sooner or later, however, questions arise that today we
would express in terms such as: "What precisely does
'biggest and strongest' mean?" It cannot mean, for instance,
simply the man with the strongest arm or firmest grip; nor
can it even mean the man with the surest aim in throwing
his spear. The "biggest and strongest" might mean, rather,
the most cunning or ruthless. The definition would surely
include, at any rate, cunning and stealth, nimbleness and
agility. It should include everything that makes for
efficiency in achieving the tribal aim. The man who so
succeeds, winning the tribal acclamation, succeeds because
he has in one way or another gathered into himself power of
one kind or another, be it kingcraft or priestcraft.

Hence, of course, the familiar political fact that, when
you elect a man to public office for the usual political
reasons, you should recognise that the qualities of strength
and power that you have admired and for which you have
elected him are such as equip him to use his power against
you as well as for you. Once you have elected him, the very
factors of ambition and self-seeking that have made you
elect him in the first place are just those factors that will

make him more likely to use you than to serve you. If, as usually occurs, you fail to awaken quickly enough to what your tyrant is doing to you, you will continue to worship in him the very qualities that made you put him on the throne in the first place, which of course you have immeasurably encouraged and enlarged by your putting him there. You will worship his power and his strength. You need not be particularly primitive to fall into that trap. When I was in Germany in 1938, the year before the outbreak of World War II, all suggestions that the Führer might lack any of the qualities that were to be expected in a Führer and are usually associated with deity were waved off with a smile and the triumphant assertion, uttered with much rolling of the eyeballs, "Er ist *da*," with an untranslatably Germanic stress on the *da*. That Hitler was this or that seemed to have receded into a psychological limbo. The one fact that mattered, the one fact that counted, was: he is *there;* he is in the saddle. You might perhaps wish, on the side, to engage in the private worship of this or that object of your emotions, since it is always a good thing to get cathartic treatment of these encumbrances; but unless you are insane you will publicly worship Power. You will worship it with all your heart and with all your soul, and with such mind as you may have left by the time you have used up the rest of your equipment.

Bertrand Russell, in a book entitled *Power*, undertook to prove that "the fundamental concept in social science is Power, in the same sense in which Energy is the fundamental concept in physics." [1] He went on to say that while power takes many forms (wealth, armaments, civil authority, influence on opinion, and so forth) none of these can be accounted subordinate to any other, nor is there any form from which the others may be said to be derived. Sometimes military power has been isolated and exalted above all other

[1] Bertrand Russell, *Power* (London: George Allen and Unwin, Ltd., 1938), p. 10.

forms of power, as if victory or defeat depended upon the commanders. More commonly, at any rate at the time Russell was writing between the wars, economic power was taken to have that supreme place among the forms of power. There is in fact, however, no more a kind of power that is supreme than there is such a form of energy: "power, like energy, must be regarded as continually passing from any one of its forms into any other. . . . The attempt to isolate any one form of power, more especially, in our day, the economic form, has been and still is, a source of errors of great practical importance." [2]

Russell was, I am convinced, successful in defending that thesis, and we see his success corroborated all around us. Moreover, the insight he so well expresses here is one that primitive peoples enjoyed in their own way. In the history of religion we find the insight clearly expressed in the focusing of naked power in deity. That may be historically the most developed form of anthropomorphism. If so, it is also the most persistently idolatrous. If such religion were to develop along purely naturalistic lines it would learn to worship, not *mana* or electricity or radium or fission but energy itself. Since a pure nature-worship is seen by most people to be inadequate or unsatisfactory, the object of worship that emerges is not so much "Pure Energy" as "Naked Power." Of course, since both science and metaphysics are latecomers to the human scene, people do not usually specify the object of their worship with such intellectual precision. Around deity cluster a variety of old idolatries that have to be somehow or other incorporated into the total picture of God. Not only, for instance, does he sit on a throne with the sceptre of power in his right hand; he must also be wise, so he is bearded (for beards at one time symbolized age, and age was identified with wisdom), and he must also appear benign, so his countenance must be

[2] Ibid., pp. 11f.

marked by an expression of serenity and beneficence. Sometimes he may have to be depicted with an accent on this quality, sometimes with an emphasis on that.

In Mahayana Buddhism, for example, such variations are achieved by the convenient device of changing the position of the Buddha's fingers so as to present him in his teaching or meditative or other aspects, as the situation may seem to require. The quality of power, however, is always, to say the least, foremost. A powerless deity is assumed to be useless to everybody. Even the most primitive peoples recognize that. When, for example, the rain-god fails them, they may first of all remonstrate with him ("Please, dear god, allow us to remind you"); then they may shake him or even give him a good whipping; then finally, when all else seems to fail they assume his power has gone and accordingly they fire him. Rain is the value they expect of him, and he has proved himself, after reasonable trial, powerless to produce it. He must be liquidated. One cannot go on indefinitely employing a god who is powerless. Being powerless, he is literally useless. Who could want a useless god?

Great twentieth-century dictators such as Lenin, Mussolini, and Hitler, to mention only the departed, not only had all the somewhat repulsive qualities usually needed for success in democratic politics; they owed their rise to democratic processes. In due course, all such dictators fall, though not usually before they have brought incalculable human suffering in their train. Idols of the people who admire them for their power and invest them with a still larger panoply of it, they turn out, in the end, to be powerless for the task entrusted to them because they have so abused their power that it has turned in upon themselves and destroyed them. According to the psalmist, what was wrong with the idols of the Egyptians and other heathen deities was not that they were wicked or cruel or lustful but that they were powerless: they

> *have mouths, but never speak,*
> *eyes, but never see,*

> *ears, but never hear,*
> *noses, but never smell,*
> *hands, but never touch,*
> *feet, but never walk,*
> *and not a sound from their throats.*
> *Their makers will end up like them,*
> *and so will anyone who relies on them.*
> *House of Israel, rely on Yahweh,*
> *on him our help and shield.*
>
> . . . .
>
> *Heaven belongs to Yahweh,*
> *earth he bestows on man.*[3]

The heathen gods are denigrated because they are powerless; Yahweh is to be praised because

> *Ours is the God whose will is sovereign*
> *in the heavens and on the earth.*[4]

The whole Hebrew preoccupation with power was transmitted to primitive Christianity. The prophets had seen an ethical dimension in God; but most people saw that dimension overshadowed by his power. Moreover, the Hebrews, unlike the Greeks, had no conception of Nature. They had not even a word for it. The New Testament writers, though in theory they could have benefited from Greek speculation on Nature, had in fact no interest in it, if they had any knowledge of the concept. They were heirs to the Hebrew rather than the Greek view. One of their most striking preoccupations was with miracle, which in Greek is commonly designated *dynamis*, a Greek word meaning literally "power." It is so understood in our own Greekless society that admires, in business, the "dynamic" salesman and, in the Church, the "dynamic" priest.

---

[3] Ps. 115:5–9, 16 (JB).
[4] Ps. 115:3 (JB).

Through the Incarnation, the power of God enters into the world. The power of God overshadows Mary and she conceives a child by the power of the Holy Ghost.[5] Jesus *is* the power of God.[6] The Gospel itself is called the power of God.[7] The woman who touched the skirt of Jesus plainly expected power to flow through or from it as surely as I expect juice to flow from an electric power station to my desk lamp.[8] After the Ascension the power of God inheres in the Church.[9] At Pentecost the power of God descends upon the apostles.[10] These are among the great miracles of the Christian story; but the miracles performed by Jesus are, of course, *dynameis* too. Indeed, an understanding of the meaning of the New Testament miracles is impossible except by seeing them as functions of the power of God. Jesus exhibits the power of God and, in the end, on the Day of Judgment, he shall return again and show it forth in its plenitude. Hitherto he has mercifully diluted it; then it shall be seen unveiled, and all creation shall quake at the sight. It is not to be naked or capricious; it is to be allied to justice, for Jesus is to return in the role of the Just Judge of all the earth, rectifying all moral wrongs, laying wicked usurpers low and establishing righteousness instead of the reign of unrighteousness as hitherto. But it is to be "clout." The only difference seems to be that the good news that is the "clout" happens to be vested in a Just Judge rather than in wicked princes. Apart from that, the difference between God and Zeus is not as striking as one might expect. The whole Christian story, as it has been popularly understood, is indeed an extension and special interpretation of the completion of the panorama of Hebrew history.

[5] Luke 1:35.
[6] 1 Cor. 1:24; Cf. Matt. 28:18.
[7] Rom. 1:16; 1 Cor. 1:18.
[8] Mark 5:30.
[9] Mark 9:1.
[10] Acts 1:8.

In the other great religions of the world the same power-worship continues also to be promulgated. Allah is compassionate, and good Muslims are glad of it; nevertheless, it would not be difficult to show that the prime reason for worshipping Allah is, in popular Muslim understanding, his power. The will of Allah is conceived as an infinite degree of the despotic power that is all too familiar in human society. The political despot occasionally (or frequently as the case may be) loses his temper. He often has to go on diplomatic or other missions to preserve his power. All that, however, only goes to show how far his power falls short of that of Allah who, like Zeus, need not even nod, since he can accomplish his will simply by the act of willing.

But what of the specifically Christian notion of *agapē*? With all our talk of power, have not we lost sight of it? Does not it so transform power as to make what I have said of the Christian tradition an absurd travesty and caricature? The Swedish theologian Anders Nygren, in an interesting and much-criticized study[11] in which he considers the Christian idea of love, attempts to show that the *agapē* revealed in the Gospels is a radically different *kind* of love from the *erōs* of the pagan world. That the term *erōs* is never used in the New Testament, while the term *agapē* is used in it abundantly, cannot be denied. The verb *agapaō*, however, is well known in classical Greek and means "to love" not only in the sense of regarding someone with affection but also in the straightforward sense of "to caress," being used also, moreover, in respect of non-personal relationships, in the sense of being well pleased or delighted that a certain state of affairs prevails. It therefore cannot be accounted an entirely novel Christian notion totally disconnected with *erōs*.

[11] Anders Nygren, *Agape and Eros*, trans. P. S. Watson (London: S.P.C.K., 1953). The original English edition appeared (Part I) in 1932 and (Part II) in 1938 and 1939.

Nygren, however, insists on contrasting them as sharply as faith and knowledge (*pistis* and *gnōsis*). Following the lead of R. Reitzenstein, he supposes "a formula current among the Corinthians, consisting of four members, *pistis*, *alētheia* (*gnōsis*), *erōs*, *elpis*—faith, truth (*gnōsis*), *erōs*, hope—to which Paul deliberately opposes his triple formula of 'faith, hope, and love [*agapē*].' These three alone abide." [12] Nygren wants to establish that the *agapē* that Paul has in mind here is love of God rather than love of neighbor. Christian *agapē*, on this view, is contrasted with *gnōsis*, which is just another name for *erōs*. The pretensions of the Gnostics are condemned as human folly, and what they take to be rational and intellectual, a great spiritual chemistry, is all merely part of that folly. Paul's hymn is a polemic against the Gnostics. The pagans had recognized mighty *erōs* at work in the quest for God. They had worshipped the unknown source (which Aristotle eventually was to see as the magnet) of that after which *erōs* hungers. They worshipped it as the only force greater than *erōs* itself. So it becomes in one way or another the personification of *erōs*, *erōs* seen under various guises (Venus, Mars, and so forth), but gathered up in the person of a deity such as Zeus. In doing so they were seeing in their own way what we would be asserting if, with some of the psychoanalysts, we were to say that the libido is essentially the same whether directed through ego drives or sex drives or any others. *Agapē* is radically different. If it comes to us at all it comes from God. It *is* God, at least in the sense that it fully characterizes him as it characterizes nothing else. Nygren also, as from all this we might expect, sees a sharp antithesis between *agapē* and reason.

That is probably, indeed, the point at which his critics, notably Professor Burnaby and Father D'Arcy, have principally balked.[13] Father D'Arcy sees Nygren's understanding

---

[12] Ibid., p. 136.

[13] E.g., John Burnaby, *Amor Dei* (London: Hodder and Stoughton, 1938), and

of God as onesided. Although it does justice to the divine initiative[14] and what Christian theologians have called "prevenient grace," it presents us with a strange paradox: according to Nygren, "Eros before the time of Plato is associated with a view of man as imprisoned in an earthly and sensual world. The divine in him longs for liberation or salvation, and in such cults as Orphism release was achieved by purification and by ecstasy. . . . But, if Nygren be right, once Eros is espoused by Plato and Platonism, a remarkable metamorphosis takes place. The mythos becomes a logos; what was essentially a wild and irrational passion is converted into an excessively rational religion." [15]

Father D'Arcy, penetrating near the heart of the difficulty, detects that what is really at issue in the Nygren controversy is the old squabble about the respective merits of reason and emotion. Citing a writer who, in his day, was typical of the reaction to the Victorian championing of what the Victorians took to be the Graeco-Roman classical ideal, and who contrasted two styles of art (the Greek favoring form and the Eastern favoring color), Father D'Arcy has little difficulty in showing the danger of such excessively facile antitheses.[16] Reason and emotion, form and color, "are never, and never can be, entirely separate." He quotes a remark of Sir Osbert Sitwell that human beings display "the identical combination of flaming pride and meek submission that in the animal world distinguishes the camel." [17] Reason and emotion cohabit in our souls as do brain and heart in our bodies; but Nygren is seen to be setting *erōs* on the "bad" side of the ledger and contriving

---

M. C. D'Arcy, S.J., *The Mind and Heart of Love* (New York: Meridian Books, 1956). On this controversy see also T. Gould, *Platonic Love* (New York: Free Press of Glencoe, 1963), pp. 6f.

[14] M. C. D'Arcy *Mind and Heart of Love*, p. 65.

[15] Ibid., p. 68.

[16] Ibid., pp. 23ff.

[17] Ibid., p. 25.

to ally it with the all-too-human dispositions and preoccupations that issue in an all-too-human and therefore futile religion. Reason is being denigrated as part of the all-too-human scene, man's futile "quest for the divine." On the good side Nygren places *agapē*, a novel and unique form of love, as alien from reason as it is from sensual passion and worldly ambition. Professor Burnaby, though his argument is differently developed and geared throughout to Augustine, raises similar objections.

I find myself very much in sympathy with Nygren's critics on these points. To make *erōs* totally irrelevant to the human response is a mistake. To range reason not only with *erōs* but with the wildest and most self-destructive human emotions is a graver error still. Nygren is taking up a stance on the same high but untenable ground on which, in a different connection, Karl Barth stood in his famous debate with Brunner in which Barth insisted that God, if he chose, could reveal himself to a cat.[18] Such writers, in the course of their polemic against the possibility of what was traditionally and misleadingly called "natural" theology, seek to make a total divorce between man's search for God and God's going forth to man. No such divorce is possible. I would say, rather, that God goes forth to his creatures in the act of abdication of power that creates them and so lets them be, and that when a creature responds to such love he responds in his whole being, which is the only way in which even God can engage in love. I think, however, that Nygren did see something (as did also Barth in his own way) that is of crucial importance not only for a better Christian theology but also for our whole understanding of the criteria for distinguishing good religion from bad. The clue lies not so much in an analysis of ambiguities in the term "love" (obvious though these be) as in a consideration of a

[18] Karl Barth, *Nein*, in E. Brunner and K. Barth, *Natural Theology* (London: Geoffrey Bles, 1946), p. 88.

fundamental and extraordinarily misleading ambiguity in the term "power" when it is used of God.

When God is seen as essentially self-humbling, self-abnegating, self-emptying (so exhibiting *par excellence* the sacrificial character of his love), the importance of the *agapē-erōs* distinction, though of course it is not destroyed, recedes. The reason-emotion squabble is also seen in a clearer light. What is wrong with the all-too-human kind of religion that protagonists of Christian orthodoxy rightly deplore (though they should remember they are not alone in deploring it) is not that it is seeking God and thinking it can find him by its own efforts, whether by studying a Gnostic chemistry of the spirit or by some other "rationalist" enterprise. What is wrong with it is that it has not been weaned from the worship of "clout." This dynamolatrous devotion can take a "Protestant" form or a "Catholic" one, a Muslim or a Confucian one. It occurs wherever God is seen as exerting human power in what the medieval philosophers would have called "an eminent degree." I know of no way in which we can determine which religions or which forms of Christianity tend most to perpetrate this dynamolatry. It occurs in all religions and all forms of Christianity, lingering on in strangely persistent ways even when one had thought its obsequies had been fully solemnized. Wherever it occurs it poisons all other categories such as emerged in the Nygren controversy.

Under the influence of this power-worship, *agapē* can look as arrogant as *erōs*, reason as silly as emotion. For an agapistic deity who seeks out man "with unhurrying chase" (in Francis Thompson's beautiful Augustinian image in *The Hound of Heaven*) could be seen as a far worse tyrant in his own way than Aristotle's divine magnet ever could be. What makes God no tyrant is his essential self-emptyingness. It is not that his kind of love is or is not different from the kinds familiar to us in our human manifestations of *erōs*. It is not that he is on the side of reason or against it, or whether he is to be reached by Dionysian or other emotional ecstasy or not. Nor is it even a question of whether God makes the move or we, since it is not really a "move" at all but a letting-be. The old controversies about these matters were not unimportant. They called attention to the point that concerns us. Now we must see beyond them by considering how the notion of the self-emptying-ness of God affects all the categories of the old controversy.

When we see God as self-emptying Being we see at the same time what it means for us to be with him or against him. *Erōs* as the name for human desire can be understood in a myriad of ways. It is a name for sensual lust; it also denotes all drives for self-fulfilment. It is an indispensable ingredient in self-respect. Without it one could not act so as to make possible the narcissistic satisfaction of contemplating oneself with equanimity. It is a drive for power. Yet it no more provides a specification of the nature of that power than an animal's instinct for self-preservation specifies the nature of life. In short, it is a neutral notion representing something in human nature that is to be tamed rather than something that is to be excised like a cancer.

But how, then, are we to see reason? In the course of the history of ideas it has notoriously changed its meaning: where we now understand reason as ratiocination, the working out of analytical arguments by syllogistic or other more modern forms of logic, the eighteenth century was inclined to see reason as a god, the deity of Deism. Some who were tolerant of religious ideas might be disposed to see Reason, together with Nature and the Grand Architect, as a sort of deistic Trinity. Reason was actually venerated, for example at the Cathedral of Notre Dame de Paris, for about a decade after the French Revolution. It was presented as a symbol of the highest and best in humanity, bringing salvation from what was taken to be the soul-destroying follies and idle superstitions of a dying obscur-antism, the enemy of the Enlightenment that was to exalt civilized man and so give him dominion over all possible rivals. That kind of deification of reason is echoed in the Victorian Sir Richard Burton's claim that it is "Life's sole arbiter, the magic labyrinth's single clue." That, in turn, was a very different understanding of reason from the one we find in the Greek philosophers who praised it. They gave it so large an interpretation as to identify it with practically everything that we might call "on the side of the angels." That is to say, they identified it with everything that is "intrinsically good," being good irrespective of whether we are there to admire it or choose to admire it or not.

How then are we to understand the place of reason in religion? Is it, as Sophocles called it, "the choicest gift bestowed by heaven," [19] or is it the snare it was seen to be by Pascal long before twentieth-century existentialism exhibited its weakness? Even during the *Aufklärung* the weakness of reasoning did not go unnoticed:

> *Who reasons wisely is not therefore wise;*
> *His pride in reas'ning, not in acting lies.*[20]

Men can abuse reason; but so also, God knows, they can abuse religion. So also they deify any idol of their choosing. We have no more cause, however, to list reason with God's adversaries because it is liable to abuse than we have to outlaw science because scientists have made discoveries that could harm humanity. We do not outlaw mathematics because Descartes tended to deify it. We must learn to see that neither *erōs* nor reason is at war with God any more than is human freedom itself. To say the least, reason is eminently qualified for enlistment in God's service.

What is at enmity with God in its very nature is the gratification of power-mania. For if the conclusion we

[19] Sophocles, *Antigone* 683: *Phrenas, pantōn os' esti ktēmatōn hypertaton.*
[20] Alexander Pope, *Moral Essays*, I, 117.

reached about the nature of God is true, all exercise of power as we understand it in human relations is intrinsically evil because it is fundamentally opposed, not merely to this or that divine precept or commandment that may have come to us by way of Moses or the Code of Hammurabi, but to the nature of Being itself. If God is self-abnegating, only that power that we have called kenotic or self-emptying can in any way serve the purposes of God. To talk of "kenotic power" is, indeed, an intentional paradox, like talking of a plan to mobilize for peace or praying to God in the words of the ancient collect, *cui servire regnare est:* whom to serve is to reign.

Much of the infatuation with oriental religions that we find in contemporary Western society, not least among young people, springs from a disenchantment with the popular concept of God, whose despotic image has over-shadowed what the doctrine of the Trinity was formulated to display. Augustinian answers to problems that trouble the contemporary mind, though they may mitigate some of the difficulties, are unconvincing to most people, even to those who attend to them with some diligence. They are unconvincing, not because they are wrong answers or because they go too far but because they do not go far enough. Augustine in the *De libero arbitrio* and elsewhere shows some of the consequences of the freedom that every relationship of love entails; but he still does not sufficiently show the extent of these entailments. His difficulty with the problem of the changeableness of creatures and the un-changeableness of God, which we noted in an early chapter, would have hampered his exploration of the entailments of love. A contemporary theologian expresses the misgivings of many on this point: "To love is to accept another who makes his own decisions, including that of the loving relationship itself. In loving I make the history of another's freedom my history. The refusal to accept the other's freedom to be and to decide is a failure in love, for we deny that in the other which is essential to love itself." [21] The freedom that love entails is as awesome as the love that bestows it.

What we should see in God, then, is One whose nature is to create and who, in being what he is, is ever engaged in self-abnegation. The notion of a God who could be happy and unconcerned without his creation or who "had been" in such a state before he undertook to engage in the creative enterprise becomes nonsense that nobody need try to justify, since with Origen we must see God as ever-creating. To envisage God as deciding to engage in this or that creative act once or many times is an anthropomorphism of the most misleading kind. It is based on the radically false presupposition that God exercises the kind of power that we exercise, and that he chooses to exercise it once or many times, as a war lord chooses to wage war once in his reign or thrice.

To suggest that, if God is ever-creating, then he "needs" to create is somewhat like asking whether I "need" to live. Only prospective suicides ask that question and then only about themselves. If I am healthy and happy I shall account the question silly because, though theoretically I could commit suicide, the notion of my committing it is so far from my mind that I would not entertain it for a moment. Since God is, *ex hypothesi*, everlastingly "healthy and happy," the "question" turns out to be a pseudo-question. Were you to point out to me that by being healthy and happy I cause other people to be invigorated by my health and cheered by my happiness and to go on to ask whether I "needed" their invigoration or their cheering would be, to say the least, to underestimate if not misunderstand the spontaneity of my influence. Aristotle's genius enabled him

[21] D. D. Williams, *The Spirit and the Forms of Love* (New York: Harper and Row, 1968), p. 116.

to see and express, in his own way, at least, the truth that is at issue here: God needs nothing from his creation.

When we are able to see God as creating through self-abnegation, through the self-sacrifice that love always entails, we can better understand the nature of affirmative human response to divine creativity. Of course it requires what Tillich called "the courage to be," for as my health and happiness might annoy hypochondriacs, so of course God's existence and nature annoy many. But when we do respond in love to the self-emptying God, we do so not merely by a nod or a bob or a hosanna or an amen but by our own self-abnegating acts. Simone Weil goes so far as to say: "We participate in the creation of the world by decreating ourselves. . . . May God grant that I may become nothing." [22] I think we must not take her literally, that we annihilate ourselves. On the contrary, she is providing us with the basis for a theology of creativity. She is saying that only by emptying myself can I in any way participate in the life of God, who is the plenitude of Being; nevertheless, whenever I do engage in kenotic acts, I am not only yielding myself up to God but am actually engaging with God in creation. Few have seen so well as have Kierkegaard and Simone Weil the creative role of self-abnegation. It is the secret behind the gospel paradox that I must give up my life to gain it.

Self-emptying, the principle of the kenotic Being of God, is the law of life. To disobey it by exercising such sultanic power as God allows Satan to give me does not necessarily cause my death: by such strategy I may survive, but only as a roach or a fungus. In so surviving I renounce what the gospel calls "life eternal," the *zoē* that is achieving participation in the everlastingly creative *zoē* of God. Once we attain that insight, all the old paradoxes about grace and

[22] Simone Weil, *Gravity and Grace* (London: Routledge and Kegan Paul, 1947), p. 80.

freewill recede, if they do not immediately dissolve. There is
nothing more paradoxical about them than there is in the
upanishadic doctrine of the role of free will within the
inexorable moral law of karma. What impedes our progress
in penetrating the secret is our reluctance, however unconscious, to give up the old power models of deity and
therefore of goodness, metaphysical, and moral. These dog
the steps of our thinking as persistently and often as
unwittingly as the old categories of substance and causation
dogged the thinking of Descartes long after he thought he
had renounced all traditional encumbrances.

Since such is the vision of God that our kenotic view
entails, the old "rock" imagery, serviceable though it has
been in the past, should yield to other, more useful figures.
It is misleading. In no way is God either unconcerned as is a
rock or immutable as we like to take a rock to be. God, far
from being impassible, is ever-agonizing in his self-emptying. Yet these old models were not by any means wholly
false, for such is God's creative love that it is, as we might
say, not only "as impregnable as a rock" but, rather,
infinitely more so, since no dynamite or even atomic blast
could ever touch it. And if by impassibility we mean that
God's love cannot be undermined by anything outside itself,
we may accept the notion without protest. The one ancient
model that is thoroughly and dangerously misleading is the
model of sultanic power, for it leads straight to dynamolatry. Whatever God is is so radically antithetical to that kind
of power that the use of the word "power" is calculated to
damage any vision we might enjoy and hinder any progress
we might make in achieving its enjoyment.

The use of "power" *(potestas)* as a symbol of deity is open
to the same kind of objection as is the continued use of
"authority" *(auctoritas)*. They are both very much pagan
Roman terms, having all the legal and administrative
connotations that Rome has bequeathed to us. Their use
vitiated not only any understanding we might hope to have

of the nature of creativity but every insight we might hope to achieve about the divine nature. Authority *(auctoritas)* is so fundamentally associated with the power *(potestas)* of the state and symbolized in the *fasces*, that it is difficult for even an erudite and thoughtful person to divest it of such significance and see "authority" as a means of expressing that which *morally* "commands" (or should so "command") our "obedience." Since that authority *derives* from the sultanic power *(potestas)* that lies behind it and without which it ceases to be, "power" is such an extraordinarily unfortunate symbol for anything that can be predicated of God as to be much worse than inadequate or misleading. We may allow terms such as "just" and "compassionate" to function in analogies about God because we think we can say that, despite all the agnosticism about God that is characteristic of deeply religious people, we can more fittingly and usefully call God just than we can call him unjust. Misleading as it is to call God kind, we had rather call him kind than dub him cruel. The power-predicate, however, is so singularly inapposite that calling God powerful is really less illuminating than calling him powerless.

Simone Weil, indeed, who presses both her thought and her language hard to get across her most crucial ideas (as did Kierkegaard and, of course, Paul), talks of loving the *all-powerless* God.[22] To represent God to oneself as all-powerful is to represent oneself to oneself in a state of false divinity. Man is only able to be one with God by uniting himself to God *stripped of his divinity*, emptied of his divinity.[23] She teaches that God loves in us the "consent we show in withdrawing in order to allow him to pass, in the same way as he himself, the Creator, has withdrawn in order to allow us to be." [24] If instead of exercising our power

---

[22] Simone Weil, *The Notebooks of Simone Weil*, 2 vols., trans. A. Wills (New York: G. P. Putnam's Sons, 1956), Vol. I, p, 284.

[23] Ibid.

[24] Ibid., Vol. II, p. 401.

to impede God, we withdraw, yielding to let him pass, we appropriate the fullness of the kenotic Being who "forsakes his throne" and squeezes himself into a womb and a crib and a stable and dwells with us in silence so as to let us be.

> *I come in the little things,*
> *Saith the Lord:*
> *My starry wings*
> *I do forsake,*
> *Love's highway of humility to take:*
> *Meekly I fit my stature to your need.*
> *In beggar's part*
> *About your gates I shall not cease to plead—*
> *As man, to speak with man—*
> *Till by such art*
> *I shall achieve My Immemorial Plan,*
> *Pass the low lintel of the human heart.*[25]

The green light can never turn for the "traffic of Jacob's ladder" that is "Pitched betwixt Heaven and Charing Cross" [26] till we bend low enough to let God pass as he is bending all heaven to let our little ladder reach it.

We can now also see the Satanic myth in a clearer light. Had Satan's theology been more accurate he could not even have contemplated his rebellion. He did so only because he worshipped a false divinity and, coveting it, sought to oust it. So he hurled himself to hell. He had never even "seen" God, and he still leads the power-worshippers in their common blindness. They are cosmic losers because they have never known the nature of Being. If, as I have tried to show, Being is ever self-abnegating, we in our self-abnega-

[25] Evelyn Underhill, *Immanence*, in *Poems of Today: Second Series* (London: Sidgwick and Jackson, 1922), pp. 160f.

[26] Francis Thompson, *The Kingdom of God*, in *The Oxford Book of Christian Verse* (Oxford: Clarendon Press, 1940), p. 516. Cf. Rev. 3:20: "Behold, I stand at the door and knock. . . ."

tion can be "equal to God" *in that respect*, however puny our scale. The application of all this to chastity (restraint in the use of our sexual power) is too obvious to need exposition.

Though God is properly seen as ever-creating, creativity does not exhaust the nature of his Being. God is also properly, *but not separately*, designated Being. As Being he fulfils all that has ever been worshipped in him in respect of the "supportive" or "undergirding" function anciently attributed to him; but because Being is ever-creative it is also self-emptying and therefore ever-anguished. Yet while creativity, as we have seen, entails anguish it is also, of course, joy. We may say, therefore, that God as Being is also ever-joyous in his self-emptying. Plainly, all such predicates are fraught with danger, being subject to the same limitations as are all other human predicates. Nevertheless, they are better pointers to the nature of God than is power, the most misleading symbol of all when we try to describe him whose nature is such as to be both the Good Friday love and the Easter joy that are at the core of all existence.

The use of the Greek term *agapē* to designate both the love that pervades the Church when she is truly functioning as the unique instrument of God may be convenient. Yet it has been much overworked, especially where, as so often, its use has been extended to designate the love that is in God sharply contradistinguished from all human love. For it suggests that there are two separate kinds of love, not "one good, the other better," as in Augustine's vision of the City of God, but one necessarily hostile to the other. As a way of exhibiting the difference between the Household of Faith on the one hand and, on the other, societal constructs lacking its peculiar character, calling the one the domain of *agapē* and the other the city of *erōs* would be unimpeachable. That is what Augustine did, in his way, and in so doing provided Western Europe, in the Middle Ages, with a marvelous political safeguard against Byzantine totalitarianism. When, however, theologians start composing ledgers of value in the old Pythagorean manner, listing goods on one side and evils on the other, and go on to adapt such a schema to God and man, confidently putting *agapē* on the divine side and *erōs* on the human, and arguing where to put reason and the rest, they are inviting a call for the use of Occam's razor: do not use many terms where fewer will do. For through human longings we learn, slowly and painfully though it be, that all love that entails any kind of relationship, any kind of authentic involvement with other persons, has already begun, at least, to entail self-sacrifice. To look into human love in the anguish of its self-emptying and the joy of its victory is surely, to say the least and to say it with an echo of Bonaventure's language, to be looking at the *vestigia* of God.

That is where the disciples of Bonhoeffer are right. For they see, as he saw so well, that to perceive and appreciate the greatness in human relations is the surest way of seeing what God is like. If we are to use the simplest metaphor of all, which is often the best when we try to talk of God, I would favor the Catholic imagery of the Sacred Heart. If the seventeenth-century Cardinal Bérulle was right in calling Christ "the major sacrament," that image is sacramental *par excellence.* I would carry it further, however, putting the Heart not in the breast of Jesus but at the deep core of him who has been traditionally designated the Triune God. As every human heart that knows the creative anguish of self-emptying love is a heart that beats, however feebly, with the Heart of God, so we can behold in the midst of the stream of human life the intimations of that self-emptyingness of Being that not only "moves the sun and the other stars" but cares infinitely for the sigh of the poor man whom Kierkegaard saw "walking down the High Street."

Index

Abbott, Lyman, 6
Abraham, 47
Actus purus, 13, 128
Adam, 137, 142
Adeimantus, 34
Aeschylus, 31
Agamemnon, 34
Agapaō, 174
Agapē, 9f., 159, 174ff., 187
'*Ahab*, 7
Akdamuth, 130n.
Alacoque, Margaret Mary, 77
Alētheia, 175
Alexander the Great, 124
Allah, 74, 174
Allen, R. E., 35n.
Altizer, T., ix
Angst, 17
Anselm, 13
Apocalypse, 73
Apocatastasis, 138
Aquinas, Thomas. See Thomas
    Aquinas.
Arianism, 14, 46
Arianism, Crypto-, 65
Aristotle, 33, 37, 54, 115, 175, 178,
    182
Arnold, Matthew, 162
Ascension, 173
Ateleutēton, 32
Athene, 28
Athens and Jerusalem, 42
Auctoritas and *potestas*, 184f.
Aufklärung. See Enlightenment.
Aulén, Gustav, 87

Augustine, 39ff., 46ff., 54f., 88f.,
    115, 120, 127f., 131, 133, 139,
    177, 181, 187

Bacon, Francis, ix
Baillie, Donald M., 69ff., 82
Baillie, John, 92
Barth, Karl, 52, 177
Beare, W., 70
Bérulle, Cardinal, 188
Bethlehem, 149, 166
Bhakti, 65
Biedermann, 82
Binity, 46
Bodhisattvas, 107
Boethius, 130
Bonaventure, 188
Bonhoeffer, Dietrich, 17, 134, 188
Bowie, W. R., 86n.
Brabant, F. H., 104f.
Brahman, 45
Bright, William, 79
Brightman, Edgar Sheffield, 99
Bruce, A. B., 68n.
Brunner, Emil, 177n.
Buber, Martin, 61
Buddha, 171
Buddhism, 31n., 60, 106
Bulgakov, S., 70f., 104
Bultmann, Rudolf, 81
Burnaby, John, 175, 177
Burton, Sir Richard, 180

Cadbury, H. J., 67
Calvary, 126, 149